UPCOMING EVENTS

More info on these & upcoming events at HopeHill.com/events or near the coffee table.

TODAY | KIDS CHURCH!

What: Hope Hill warmly invites you and your child to visit and experience a Hope Hill Kids Church this Sunday! It is our goal for the Hope Hill Kids Church to help your child experience extraordinary fun and meaningful learning while at church each Sunday. As a growing congregation, our Kids Church is comprised of young children of various ages, creating a fun multi-age classroom. Learn more about the Preschoolers curriculum, Mommy & Me, and safety polices at HopeHill.com/kids-church or visit the Kids Church area and pick up a brochure.
When: Every Sunday after worship, 11:30am-12:30pm
Location: First Floor Theater Entrance Lobby

FRI - FEB 1 | GETTING TO KNOW YOU DINNER @ PASTOR BEAU & RENATA'S PLACE

What: Church is so much more than the 90-minute service on Sundays. In fact, church was always meant to be a community rather than an event. We cordially invite you to come over to our apartment for a home-cooked meal and some good conversation. Swing over after work on a Friday evening and enjoy the company of your friends from Hope Hill church over dinner.
When: This Friday, February 1, 7:00-9:30pm
Location: Pastor Beau & Renata's Apartment, Downtown Brooklyn (RSVP for address)
Contact: Renata (Renata@HopeHill.com or 608-609-8400)

SAT - FEB 2 | HOPE HILL PARENTS GROUP

Calling All Parents: Parents, what an opportunity we have to raise children up to become people of values, faith, and courage in their generation. We know the greatness we envision for our children as we raise them from birth to adulthood, but we don't always feel we have all the tools we need to help our kids make it from here to there. **Low Pressure Parenting Group:** This round the parents of Hope Hill will be meeting for an hour over Zoom video every other Saturday morning to discuss concepts from the renowned parenting book *Shepherding a Child's Heart* by Tedd Tripp. Imagine this: You brew some morning coffee and breakfast, grab your book, wrap up in a blanket on the couch, and log on via video chat with Pastor Beau and Renata Lee and the other parents of Hope Hill. One hour of low-pressure discussion on a chapter from the book.
When: Saturdays February 2, 16, March 2, 16, and 30 from 10:00-11:00am
Location: Zoom video chat from the convenience of your home
Contact: Pastor Beau (Beau@HopeHill.com or 347-703-7800)
RSVP: At the sign-up table, or online at HopeHill.com/events to

SUN - FEB 3 | PIZZA LUNCH & HOPE HILL PHOTO SHOOT

What: Everyone is invited to join the pizza party immediately after the service gets over next Sunday, February 3rd. We're updating the Hope Hill website with photos of singles, couples, and families so we can show potential Sunday visitors more of who we are, and what our community is all about. It's also a great opportunity for you to get some professional, high resolution head shots with professional backdrop, lighting and camera. Eat pizza while you wait for your turn!
When: Next Sunday, February 3, immediately after church gets out

EVENTS CONTINUED

More info on these & upcoming events at HopeHill.com/events or near the coffee table.

SUN - FEB 10 | MEN'S MONTHLY CASUAL HANGOUT: LOMBARDI'S PIZZA (LITTLE ITALY)

What: Join the guys from Hope Hill Church after our Sunday church service for a men's get-together where we'll catch-up over some good grub at Lombardi's Pizza — America's oldest pizza joint. Invite your friends and join the group for lunch as we enjoy the food, get into some meaningful conversation, and build friendships that genuinely improve each other's effectiveness as men of faith. Don't miss it!
When: Sunday, February 10, 1:30-3:00pm
Location: Lombardi's Pizza (32 Spring Street, New York, NY 10012)
Bring: Cash for Lunch
Contact: Pastor Beau (Beau@HopeHill.com or 347-703-7800)

FRI - MAR 8 | EXPLORING OPTIONS FOR INFERTILITY WORKSHOP

What: Parenthood is one of the most beautiful experiences in this world, but today, for various reasons, many couples struggle with infertility. Hope Hill Church is offering a helpful workshop that gives some practical tips for your journey to overcome infertility in a God-honoring way. While there are genuine cases where children may never be in the picture, many times there are steps that can be taken that will lead to pregnancy. For many couples struggling with infertility, all that is needed is a clear picture of where to go next in the search for answers. We invite you to this workshop if you and your spouse are struggling with achieving a pregnancy. Perhaps you will hear something that will help.
When: Friday, March 8, 7:00-8:30pm
Location: The Kind's College (56 Broadway, New York, NY 10004, Classroom 625)
Cost: Free (Donations for Facility Rental Accepted)
Instructors: Pastor Beau & Renata Lee
Bring: Your spouse and some friends who may be interested
Contact: Pastor Beau (Beau@HopeHill.com or 347-703-7800)

VOLUNTEER

Name

Email   Phone

I'm interested in volunteering in the following area(s):

- ☐ Sunday Setup/Teardown
- ☐ Hospitality & Greeting Team
- ☐ Graphic Design

- ☐ Administration
- ☐ Help with Events
- ☐ Drama/Skits/Acting

- ☐ Marketing
- ☐ Other:

Please fill out and place in the offering box by the sign-up table. Thank you!

WELCOME TO HOPE HILL CHURCH
Real Faith. Real Friends. Positive Culture.

CONTACT

www.HopeHill.com
Info@HopeHill.com
(347) 703-7800

FOLLOW US

#hopehillnyc

- Facebook
- Instagram
- Twitter
- MeetUp

OUR VALUES

Great Commission — *Gospel & Discipleship*

The Two Dailies — *Prayer & Bible Reading*

The Two Weeklies — *Gather at Sunday & Midweek Meetings*

Real Community — *Get to Authentically Know Each Other*

Biblical literacy — *Know the Bible Cover to Cover*

PASTOR BEAU LEE

Beau is a professional guitarist, entrepreneur, business consultant, author of *Jesus Plus Nothing Equals Salvation*, and the Lead Pastor of Hope Hill. After studying theology at Trinity Evangelical Divinity School (TEDS), he went on to pursue a Master of Science in Management, Strategy & Leadership at Michigan State University (Broad School of Business). Pastor Beau is presently working on a Doctor of Ministry program in Growing & Multiplying Churches from Biola University (Talbot School of Theology). Beau's hobbies are studying the Bible, traveling, and walks with friends.

TITHES & OFFERINGS

Hope Hill is a members-supported congregation. Your tithes and generous donations help cover monthly expenses and help fulfill the Great Commission in our city and world.

HOW TO GIVE

- ONLINE: HopeHill.com/give

- GIVING ENVELOPE: Give w/ cash, or fill out checking, debit/credit information & place envelope in giving box.

- Text amount you want to give to 347-215-3255 (connected to Hope Hill's online giving platform) then follow the prompts.

CONNECT CARD

Please fill out and give to a Hope Hill representative.

Name _____

Email _____ Phone _____

Prayer Requests: _____

_____

JESUS
PLUS NOTHING EQUALS
SALVATION

By Beau Lee

MIND
MASSIVE
PUBLISHING

Library of Congress Cataloging-in-Publication Data is Available
ISBN-13: 978-0-9992669-0-8
ISBN-10: 0-9992669-0-X
ISBN-13: 978-0-9992669-1-5 (ebook)
ISBN-10: 0-9992669-1-8 (ebook)

Cover Design By Vlad Nicolaescu

Printed in the United States of America
First Printing 2017

Published by Mind Massive Publishing (Edition 1B)
Brooklyn, NY, USA

Author Info

Beau Lee is Founder and Lead Pastor of Hope Hill Church (www.HopeHill.com) located in New York City. Beau and Renata Lee lead tours to Israel through Israel Bible Trips (www.IsraelBibleTrips.com). Beau is available for speaking engagements, media interviews, workshops, and debates.

Ordering Information

Quantity sales. Special quantity discounts are available when purchased in bulk by churches, ministries, corporations, organizations, special-interest groups, and others. Custom imprinting or excerpting can also be done to fit special needs.

For details, contact the author.

Bible Versions

Scripture quotations marked ESV are taken from The Holy Bible, English Standard Version. ® Text Edition: 2016. ESV Copyright © 2001 by Crossway Bibles, a publishing ministry of Good News Publishers. Used by permission. All rights reserved.

Scripture quotations marked NASB are taken from The Holy Bible, New American Standard Bible. Copyright © 1960, 1962, 1963, 1968, 1971, 1973, 1975, 1977, 1995 by The Lockman Foundation. Used by permission. All rights reserved.

Scripture quotations marked NKJV are taken from The Holy Bible, New King James Version. Copyright © 1982 by Thomas Nelson, Inc. Used by permission. All rights reserved.

Scripture quotations marked NIV are taken from The Holy Bible, New International Version. Copyright © 1973, 1978, 1984, 2011 by Biblica, ® Inc. Used by permission. All rights reserved worldwide.

Scripture quotations marked NLT are taken from the Holy Bible, New Living Translation. Copyright © 1996, 2004, 2007, 2013, 2015 by Tyndale House Foundation. Used by permission of Tyndale House Publishers, Inc., Carol Stream, Illinois 60188. All rights reserved.

ABOUT THE AUTHOR

Beau Lee is Founder and Lead Pastor of Hope Hill Church—an exciting faith community in the heart of Manhattan (NYC). As the firstborn son of a minister, Beau grew up inside the epicenter of the Christian community, gaining a behind-the-scenes view of American Christianity, its teachers, and its Gospel theology. As Beau sought answers to questions about his salvation, he realized the church was missing a unified understanding of how to get to heaven. A surprising number of church members were admittedly confused about what the Gospel was and how it "works"—and this pastor's son was no exception.

After a seven-year quest to find assurance of salvation and through a brutal defeat in his wrestling match with God's law, Beau was shocked to finally realize he had actually been a *Christian unbeliever* all along—even while filling a prominent role in the church. With God's help, Beau finally discovered grace, and it was fresh, ultra-biblical, and altogether startling.

This author understands and knows the church well. He has been as lost in the grip of guilt and self-righteousness as anyone has ever been, and he has been as fully set free from that bondage as anyone can ever be. With this experience, Beau Lee is uniquely equipped to speak to the church about the Gospel.

DEDICATION

Jesus, you deserve my infinite appreciation for taking the full weight of punishment for my sins so that I don't have to. This grace does not come cheap, and You truly emptied Your pockets for me.

Dad, thanks for teaching me to value the Bible. I learned how to live by watching you pray and study God's Word every day as I grew up. You are a true leader of the heart.

Renata—love of my life—thank you for your constant encouragement and for being the best teammate imaginable. Your edits and suggestions improved this book immensely. I'm so glad to have the opportunity to walk through the countless adventures of this life with you.

Special thanks to Martin Luther as well. Although I don't agree with all he said—especially his disparaging writings against the Jews—I am eternally grateful for those several pages of his book I read when I was twenty-three years old. His words helped me see the importance of putting my full trust in Jesus for salvation.

CONTENTS

PART 5: GOING EVEN DEEPER STILL

PART 6: CAN A BELIEVER LOSE SALVATION?

PART 7: THE THREE THINGS EVERYONE SHOULD KNOW

PART 8: CONCLUSION: THE GAME PLAN

APPENDIX A: A SALVATION CREED FOR CHURCHES

APPENDIX B: OVERVIEW OF THE GOSPEL

APPENDIX C: SALVATION VERSES OF THE NEW TESTAMENT

MY NAME IS BEAU LEE, and I am writing from my apartment in downtown Brooklyn, New York City, overlooking the Statue of Liberty. My delightful wife, Renata, and I both came to faith in our twenties, and we are now using our lives to share what we found with others. As many of you know, NYC is an ultra-exciting city, and I happen to spend much of my time pastoring a fun, energetic, and life-changing church in Manhattan: Hope Hill Church (www.HopeHill.com). The people there are amazing, and although they have moved to the city from all around the world, we have really become quite the family. Come visit us sometime, and if you are ever looking to move to the most exhilarating city in the world to help reach our diverse population, get in touch.

We've got an intensely interesting, probably controversial, and eye-opening journey ahead for many of us as we make our way through this book. I believe truth-seekers of all sorts will feel God's guidance in their life in an incredible way as they read forward—especially as we discuss the mighty truths found in the many Bible passages we will cover. If you read with expectation, something great will happen. Jesus put it this way:

> "Anyone with ears to hear should listen and understand." Then He added, "Pay close attention to what you hear. The closer you listen, the more understanding you will be

given—and you will receive even more. To those who listen to my teaching, more understanding will be given. But for those who are not listening, even what little understanding they have will be taken away from them."
Mark 4:23–25, NLT

According to Jesus' words to the people listening, if you listen with great interest and desire for truth, great truth will be poured out on you from heaven. If you listen with passivity and inattention, this is the effort heaven will use to pour truth back on you. Big input results in a big return; little input will produce little gain. That's how it works. So pay attention—especially when we read the words from the Holy Scriptures. They are waiting on these pages, ready to change your life (and maybe even your eternal destiny).

TOO MUCH CONFUSION

This book is all about the *Gospel*—God's divine plan to lovingly rescue sinners from the condemnation they deserve. Of all messages, this one should be the one ringing out from our pulpits with frequency and crystalline clarity. Yet something is wrong! Would it surprise you to hear that over 50 percent of the world's one billion church members are confused about how to get to heaven? Were you aware that a majority of global church attendees are in danger of falling for the devil's "gospel" counterfeits that are leading people to hell?

In your faith community or the one some friends or family members attend, it is likely most sitting in the pews find the Gospel to be a confusing, vague, and frustrating topic. How can I be so certain of this? Because I have surveyed many pew-sitters around this country and have analyzed the results. *We, the people of the church, are confused about the Gospel.* This should not be.

The Gospel remains an undiscovered treasure for so many. If we were to take time to have a one-on-one conversation with each of the one billion church members across the world, we'd find three distinctly different categories of people:

- **CATEGORY 1:** People who have accepted the Gospel and are saved. These people are Believers.

- **CATEGORY 2:** People who haven't yet chosen to accept the Gospel and are *not* saved. These people are Unbelievers.

- **CATEGORY 3:** People who have accepted a *false gospel*, think they are saved, but are *still not saved*. These people are still Unbelievers.

It's this significant *third* category of churchgoers that provoked me to write this book. For many of these people, the "gospel" is a vague and out-of-focus concept—some unspecified concoction of all the good and religious things they've heard about over the years. Yes, to them, attaining heaven seems to require a little bit of faith in Jesus, a good heart, some Bible reading, a pinch of prayer, and a pint of good behavior—oh, and we can't forget the truckloads of so-called "repentance." Unfortunately, this ambiguous "gospel" they are relying on to get to heaven is just a placebo, and placebos are useless to save anyone. Because of this, these countless individuals are still spiritually lost—lost right within our churches. This is why this book exists.

THE GREATEST MISSION FIELD ON THE PLANET

False representations of the Gospel make it into our churches today—and it happens far more than we might think. Paul warned a group of believers with a shout:

> I am astonished that you are so quickly deserting the One who called you to live in the grace of Christ and are turning to a different gospel—which is really no gospel at all. Evidently some people are throwing you into confusion and are trying to pervert the gospel of Christ. But even if we or an angel from heaven should preach a gospel other than the one we preached to you, let them be under God's curse! As we have already said, so now I say again: If anybody is preaching to you a gospel other than what you accepted, let them be under God's curse!
> Galatians 1:6–9, NIV

If Paul and the other apostles took up so many pages in our Bibles to refute the false gospel teaching in their churches, we should not be naïve and dismissive today. With hundreds of millions of "Christian unbelievers" out there, *the church is truly the greatest mission field on the planet.* Because of this, we desperately need to develop strong Gospel discernment in our churches.

I was once deceived by a false gospel, and my authority on this topic is well established, built firmly upon the massive theological failures of my past. Thank God, I survived the deception and lived to tell about it. Now my heart throbs for "Christian unbelievers" who are like I used to be. I want them to be free.

DIFFERENT TYPES OF READERS

I couldn't be more excited to share this book with you. Some readers already understand the Gospel with great clarity, and the value of this book will help them prioritize and clarify their Gospel presentations to the unbelievers inside and outside the church. It may also help them identify the nuances of many false gospels out there so they can help others untangle their jumbled theological balls of yarn.

Other readers may have never heard the Gospel message quite as the Bible explains it, and these people are unaware of this great saving reality. If this is you, I hope you have your mind blown by the beauty of God's rescue plan—it is truly astonishing!

There will certainly be readers who would consider themselves "Christians" but who have fallen for one of the devil's subtle counterfeits. If you fall into this group, the Gospel you have believed is the wrong path with lying signs that say "heaven" but will ultimately lead you to hell. For you, I pray this book quickly shines some refreshing light on the misguided path you are on so you can backtrack to the correct path. How refreshing it will be to feel the peace of God as you finally find yourself grounded on the assurance of your salvation.

Finally, for those who are not religious at all, you are as welcome to read this book as anyone. I am so happy to share a message with you that the Bible says will allow you to be forgiven, reconciled to the God who made you and loves you, and find an eternal home in heaven after this life is over. Read with a mind open to truth, wherever it leads, and you will have to make your choice one way or another.

SADNESS IN THE EXCITEMENT

There is one thing that makes the release of this book difficult. I grew up as a pastor's kid, and I am now pastor of a church in the heart of New York City. My heart throbs with love for Jesus' churches. I want nothing more than to see unity and peace among the many individual churches around the nation and world.

What is difficult for me is recognizing that when this book is released, it will draw a line in the sand and people will pick their sides as to what the Gospel is and isn't. I have already seen this division—even among the early readers of this manuscript. Some readers will find this book to be a breath of fresh air for the soul, while others will perceive it as scandalous. Why will there be such strong and divergent reactions? Because, as Galatians 1:6–9 said earlier, there are different false "gospels" floating around out there—yet there is only one *true* Gospel. God's will is for unity, but truth must be prioritized above unity if the choice between the two is forced. Jesus knew the division over truth and error would be inevitable, and He said:

> Do you think that I have come to give peace on earth? No, I tell you, but rather division. For from now on in one house there will be five divided, three against two and two against three. They will be divided, father against son and son against father, mother against daughter and daughter against mother, mother-in-law against her daughter-in-law and daughter-in-law against mother-in-law.
> Luke 12:51–53, ESV

What should a person do if they read the Scriptures and follow God's leading to the true Gospel, but some friends and family won't follow God's path, but instead choose a path you know to be wrong? Unity was always Jesus' will for us, but some will choose not to accept the truth, so a wise person may be required to depart from the views of those he or she loves to side with God. This can bring division of belief between two people who love each other. The first commandment is to love God with everything we have; the second is to love the people around us. Both are important, but pleasing God and following His truth must always come first.

A BOOK FOR EQUIPPING

I may not know you personally, but I have put a lot of care into this book. I really want it to be helpful for you. The pastor's role is "to equip the saints for the work of ministry, for building up the body of Christ, until we all attain to the unity of the faith and of the knowledge of the Son of God, to mature manhood, to the measure of the stature of the fullness of Christ, so that we may no longer be children, tossed to and fro by the waves and carried about by every wind of doctrine, by human cunning, by craftiness in deceitful schemes" (Ephesians 4:12–14, ESV). So here is a book that goes to great trouble to remind people—especially the church folks—the true Gospel *as the Bible teaches it* is sure to save us to the max.

You will find many Scriptures used from various translations, both literal and paraphrased versions, and each passage used is faithful to the original meaning. If a paraphrased version is used, it is used for clarity for all readers and has precise fidelity to the heart of the original text. As you read, many questions about God's salvation may arise, and this is good, and all part of the book's design. Keep reading. I encourage you to resolve in your heart to read every page because each part of this book has something completely new to offer and different questions to answer. Go to the Table of Contents and check off each chapter as you go along, and don't quit until the end of the book. I believe if you will put your heart and mind fully into this study of the Gospel, it just might be the thing that brings the most important message in the history of the universe into greater focus for you. I pray God will guide you on this adventure.

Beau Lee

For no one can lay a foundation other than
that which is laid, which is Jesus Christ.
1 Corinthians 3:11, ESV

Part 1

TENSION IN MY SOUL

Chapter 1

WILL JESUS VOMIT ME OUT OF HIS MOUTH?

L OOKING BACK TO my mid-teen years, I remember developing a deep and authentic yearning to be in a right-standing relationship with the God I knew was out there. Something within me desired to closely follow the path of truth wherever it would lead. During this wonderful time, I came to experience an organic, genuine love for the God I read about in the Bible, and I desperately wanted to learn all I could about this God and serve Him with all my heart. In the midst of the beauty of this pure thing blossoming within me, I was a young and naïve believer; I failed to notice when false teachers crept up all around me and sowed the weeds that would grow up to choke out my faith. This is the period I refer to as "my spiritual kidnapping." Let me tell you about it.

A SPIRITUAL KIDNAPPING

Being incredibly zealous for my newfound faith, I absorbed anything I could find that might help me grow in this faith. Not really having a clue how to discern truth from fallacy, I unwittingly trusted that anything with the tag "Christian" attached to it was reliable. My "kidnappers" crept in through the books people handed me, teachers on the "Christian" television channels, magazine articles, lecturers I heard, conferences, video series, and many other similar forms of communication. While not all the teachings I found were misguided, the bad teachers were subtly interwoven among the good. Such is the nature of the devil's lies: the false teachings overcome and muddle the way a person sees and understands even the true teachings. In this way, they grabbed me, bagged me, and threw me in their trunk and drove off—far away from the house of my heavenly Father. I was too young in the faith to understand what was happening, but I have since looked back at the dustier books on my bookshelf and now see what a menace they were to me.

In retrospect, I can see the primary intention of these faulty teachers and authors was to persuade me I had to make myself good enough for God if I desired to get into heaven to be with Him. These men and women believed they were doing God a favor by reforming the young. They warned us that if we ever made the mistake of allowing our commitment to Jesus to become mediocre, He would surely reject us and we wouldn't be fit to spend eternity with Him. These people often quoted Revelation 3:16 (NKJV) where Jesus declares: "Because you are lukewarm, and neither cold nor hot, will I vomit you out of My mouth." The explanation I was given for this verse went as follows: *Jesus expects you will obey Him and be fully dedicated to Him in everything you do, and if you don't do these things to the very best of your ability, He will reject you and send you to hell.* This is what my young ears heard from the instructors around me, and although my heart was as sincere as it could be, somehow, through this teaching, my gratitude and pure love for God was stripped away. How? Let me explain.

THE PURSUIT OF PERFECTION

Striving fiercely to "remain saved," I attempted to maintain a constant state of 100 percent commitment to Christian service, religious disciplines, and the lifestyle commandments in the Bible. I felt this was the only way I could stay securely within the safety of God's salvation and be found worthy of a place in heaven. After all, I believed if I didn't remain fully dedicated and rigorously obedient to Jesus in every area of my life, He would certainly "vomit" me out of His mouth. Can you imagine the incredible pressure this thinking brings? If there was ever a day I didn't fulfill this lofty level of commitment, I supposed I would probably be considered unworthy of God's presence if I happened to die that day. If I really stopped to think about it, I was never sure whether I was good enough to be saved from day to day. I would wonder, "Has my heart been pure enough today? Has my behavior been good enough to make God happy? Have I really made Jesus 'the Lord of my life' enough to be in His good graces?" When I inevitably sinned, I felt I would need to prove my commitment to Him through good behavior to get into right standing with God again. If I could perform well for a few good days, I would once again feel comforted and would say: "Look, Self, you really are committed to God. You proved it. He really is the Lord of your life."

Of course, all I am explaining of my past understanding of God and His plan for salvation is not at all a biblical understanding; instead, it's a man-made path that claims to lead to God but really leads in the opposite direction. Regrettably, though, I did what any sincere truth-seeker would do if they were told their salvation depended on their Christian devotion and obedience: I shot off on a radical journey to somehow obtain acceptance from God. Fervent vigilance in prayers, concentrated Bible reading sessions, ethical behavior, and bold so-called "evangelism" all became mile markers on the path I took to pursue salvation. I remember so clearly how the main thrusts of my prayers were, "God, create in me a clean heart. Please wrench this sin out of me! Help me to remove this garbage from my life." I was convinced that ferocious hatred of sin and boundless commitment to righteous living would do something to help me earn God's approval and somehow place me firmly on the path to heaven.

A FRUSTRATED SALVATION

I eventually learned the path I was on was a dead end. Through my late teens and into my early twenties, it became more and more evident that all my industrious work at bettering myself did nothing to help my relationship with God. Something strange happened that I never would have expected. It seemed the more I read the commandments of the Bible and learned about God's holiness, the more unachievable God's perfect standards became in my eyes. I noticed the more powerful the microscope I would use to investigate and eradicate the minutia of sin in my thoughts and inner motives, the more sin I discovered in me. For every sin I exterminated from my life, there were a thousand more that came into view. It was as if my soul's DNA was corrupted with sin. It was a disaster! The problem was I had believed the lie that Jesus would reject the humans who were "lukewarm"—those who lacked completely passionate commitment twenty-four hours a day, seven days a week. Not surprisingly, I found it impossible to sustain this pedal-to-the-medal behavior 24-7, and I was tormented as I fell in and out of the fear of being "vomited out of Jesus' mouth" for not following Him closely enough.

THEN CAME THE TRUTH

I eventually cracked under the weight of these impossible moral standards and the guilt I carried on my back. I remember going to church one Sunday morning when I was around twenty-three years old, and I told a close friend about the internal wrestling match going on inside. I asked him: "Where is the line between heaven and hell? How good do I have to be to know with certainty I'm right with God? Where is the straw that 'breaks the camel's back'—that point where if I sin once more I will be damned? I've got to know for sure if I am saved or not!" My eyes glossed over with tears as I earnestly grappled with these issues. At this point I had become spiritually exhausted from the years of striving for a salvation that seemed out of reach.

Not long after this, the truth finally hit me. I happened to walk into the movie theatre to check out a film that seemed to have some spiritual characteristics to it. Sitting down by myself, I watched a story unfold about a sixteenth-century monk named Martin Luther—a man I knew absolutely nothing about who also desperately wanted to be clean before God and to obtain His approval. There was one scene I deeply connected with where Luther was laying on the floor in his small bedroom within the monastery, fervently begging God to rip the sin out of his life and make him pure. He was crushed beneath the weight of his sin, not ever knowing with certainty whether he was safe within the protective walls of salvation or hell-bound under the condemnation of his sin. I acutely related with what I saw, knowing full well my moments of falling to the floor in my bedroom, begging God for His approval and inner cleansing. The film portrayed this man as having found a solution to his guilt, and I wanted to know what it felt like to be settled in my relationship with God.

When the movie was over, I left the theatre and drove directly to a local bookstore to look for a book by Luther. I found one entitled *By Faith Alone*.[1] I sat down in a chair toward the back of the shop, flipped open the book, and it was there that I read the following:

> When we become aware of our sin and frightened by it, we must not allow the sin to remain on our conscience. This would only lead to despair. Rather, just as our awareness of sin flowed to us from Christ, so we must pour our sin back on him to free our conscience. So be careful you don't become like the misguided people who allow their sin to bite at them and eat at their hearts. They strive to rid themselves of this sin by running around doing good works. But you have a way to get rid of your sins. You throw your sins on Christ when you firmly believe that Christ's wounds and suffering carried and paid for your sins. As Isaiah said, 'The Lord has laid all our sins on him' (Isaiah 53:6). Peter said, 'Christ carried our sins in his body on the cross' (1 Peter 2:24). And Paul said, 'God had Christ who was sinless, take our sin' (2 Corinthians 5:21). (Luther, 1998, p. 7)

As I read through the first ten pages, I could scarcely believe the wonderful things I was reading! My eyes scanned the paragraphs and Scriptures presented, and they explained the work Jesus completed on the cross was sufficient to fully cleanse us of our sin guilt once-and-for-all and fix our relationship with God—all this apart from anything we did to earn it. It declared it was through trusting in Jesus that we were saved, and not by helping our salvation along by being "good enough."

---

[1] Luther, M. (1998). *By Faith Alone*. Iowa Falls, Iowa: World Bible Publishers.

As far as I was concerned, this was news hot off the press! My eyes opened wide and my jaw dropped as I wondered within my heart, "Could it really be that everything I ever needed to be right with God and make it to heaven was already accomplished by Jesus two thousand years ago when He died on the cross? Is this what the whole Jesus-on-the-cross thing was all about? Could it really be true my salvation doesn't have anything to do with how I perform for God, but everything to do with something Jesus had already done?" As a young man who had been exhausted by years of chasing a mirage, I gasped a thousand gasps at the thought.

It was then and there in the bookstore that God revealed His jaw-dropping truth deep within my core. Up to this point, I had sought the salvation God offered, yet I had been kept from receiving it due to the flawed teaching I received. Now, as I read these pages, the assurance of salvation I had been searching and toiling for could now be immediately attained through the cross. Jesus had taken the full punishment for every one of my sins upon Himself, willfully accepting all the punishment I so completely deserved. God would consider this amazing "swap" as completely satisfactory to drop all condemnation for my sin guilt.

This amazing forgiveness and reconciliation to God had nothing to do with my behavior. In fact, this came *in spite of* my behavior. I didn't have to work to earn it. The reality was I never would be able to live up to God's perfect standards, and because of this, God offered salvation as one massive *gift* from start to finish! My salvation was secured by Jesus, and all I had to do was trust in what He had done. No wonder one of God's prophets declared: "All us, like sheep, have strayed away. We have left God's paths to follow our own. Yet the LORD laid on Him the sins of us all" (Isaiah 53:6, NLT).

As my faith mixed with these astounding truths, the door to my spiritual cage finally swung open and I was free. Without a doubt, I consider this the pivotal moment of my existence—the moment I was saved—and I owe it all to Jesus. I had spent my entire life in a variety of religious settings, yet I couldn't figure out how to be right with God. I had wrongly believed I knew the way, but I was so incredibly lost while standing right in the center of the Christian community.

Now, on that extraordinary day, I finally discovered what to trust in to be saved. Jesus died for me, taking the judgment and punishment for my sins so I never would have to be judged and punished. The innocent had died for the guilty, and the guilty man went free. Now I understood what true Christianity, the Bible, and the cross were all about! Jesus was earning the forgiveness of my sins and my right standing with God as He hung on the cross two thousand years ago, and now I finally realized it! This truth hit me for the first time in my life, crushing my false paradigms like a semi, but gently touching my heart like a warm breeze. "I can't believe it: It really *was* finished," I shouted within myself as I walked out the bookstore.

I went home and opened the Bible to read through the book of Romans, taking careful notes. It was all there. Jesus really was my Savior. I got out my journal, took a red marker, and wrote in big, bright letters: "GRACE!" From that point forward, *everything* changed. I felt utter peace in my relationship with God. I felt absolute security in my salvation. I knew if I died and had to stand before God, He would count me as righteous and give me a "ticket" into heaven. I felt anew that pure love I had felt so long ago at age sixteen. In this great new life, as I trusted in Jesus alone for my salvation, I finally came to experientially understand Jesus' wonderful words spoken to many who had been striving for right standing with God through perfection:

Come to Me, all you who labor and are heavy laden, and I will give you rest. Take My yoke upon you and learn from Me, for I am gentle and lowly in heart, and you will find rest for your souls. For My yoke is easy and My burden is light.
Matthew 11:28–30, NKJV

THE "X" THAT MARKS THE SPOT

Even as I write this eight years after my "grace" experience, I wonder how it is I could have been settled right within the Christian community for so long yet I never understood what it was all about. How could I have been so close to the church, the Holy Scriptures, and to prayers directed toward the God of the Bible, yet be so far away from salvation? How many people like me are still seeking truth with all their hearts, yet they cannot see it because false conceptual structures block their minds? I was dedicated to learning about God, to Christian service, and to behavioral reformation for seven years before I could see the truth, beauty, and simplicity of the original, true, untainted Gospel.

Imagine for a moment that our churches are made up of people searching for a priceless buried treasure. Some within our community have found it, but many among us are still searching. These seekers have shovels in their hands, hiking boots on their feet, compasses and maps in full use. The treasure chest is tucked away, only a few feet down, containing unimaginable wealth for the finder. These truth-hunters dig down here, there, and everywhere, often in close proximity to the treasure chest. Yet their shovels never quite hit the prize. As we all know, when it comes to a treasure hunt, to be *close* is not good enough. In fact, to be close is worth absolutely nothing. To experience the desired outcome, you must *fully arrive.*

So what is the "X" that marks the spot in our search for the treasure of salvation? As Luther the monk, Paul the Pharisee, Peter the Jewish fisherman, myself, and countless others throughout history have discovered, the following location is the only place where human beings will ever find the priceless treasures of God: the cross of Jesus. It is here and only here that we will finally experience the unfathomable riches of God's forgiveness, love, and restored relationship—like a giant treasure chest filled with pure gold and silver coins being emptied on our heads.

RELAX AND TRUST: THE DIFFICULT WORK OF THE CROSS IS ALREADY FINISHED

Now relax—Jesus will not spit you out of His mouth because of your shortcomings. When Jesus spoke of vomiting something out of His mouth in Revelation 3:16, He was not speaking about a human being rejected for poor performance.

Instead, He was speaking to a "lukewarm" corporate congregation of believers—the church of the city of Laodicea in the country of modern-day Turkey who had corporately failed to be a good representation of Him in their society. What is a church that verbally pushes religion but has failed to live as an example? It's simple: just another country club. Jesus warned the church of Laodicea that if they did not turn around and remember their purpose as a church was to be all about Him and His gospel, they had no right or reason to exist as an organized congregation. Jesus was not speaking about the salvation of an individual, and He certainly was not threatening to send believers to hell if they ever have a period where they get distracted from religious service or are struggling with some sin.

It's not my love for Jesus that saves me—it's His great love for me. It's not my perfect commitment to Him—it's His absolutely perfect commitment to me. All our good works, behavioral reformation, and religious service do not play any role in saving us. Instead, we are saved by the gift of salvation through the Savior, Jesus. He died for our sins, taking the full punishment upon Himself so that we wouldn't have to be punished. No, Jesus will not spit us out of His mouth if we behave poorly or are not gung-ho religious zealots every second of every day. He knew full well that we all had failed the sin test, and this is why He came to bear the cross in the first place. If you believe Jesus took the full punishment for your sins on the cross so that you don't have to, and that He resurrected from the dead, proving His death was truly ordained by God, then you are saved— sin cannot stick to your record, and no one in the world has any right to condemn you. Relax in knowing Jesus' work on the cross is *finished*.

Chapter 2

WHEN THE PURSUIT OF RIGHTEOUSNESS TURNS BLOODY

YOU'VE PROBABLY HEARD people say, "If you want to be saved, you must *repent* and *believe*." There are two things in this short set of instructions we should notice. First, *repentance* is prescribed, and the person making this demand often means the listener must turn away from all their sins. Second, belief in Jesus is prescribed. If nothing else, it all sounds pretty good and religious, doesn't it? Now let's delve into this so-called "gospel message" a little bit deeper to find out what's really going on.

"REPENTANCE" IN THE TEEN YEARS

I attended several church youth groups throughout my teen years. As an adolescent sitting in one particular group, I can attest that the primary thrust of the Gospel teaching we received went as follows:

> "Do you want to get to heaven? If so, do a 180° turn with your life by turning away from your sin and turning toward Jesus! Look and see for yourself: If you are facing toward sin,

you are not facing toward Jesus. Sin and Jesus are opposites, and you can't have both. You can choose sin if you want to, but you can't be saved then."

As fourteen, fifteen, and sixteen-year-olds, many of us were just warming up to Jesus and seeking a relationship with God, and our doctrinal foundations were essentially non-existent. With this said, our paradigms were being established with every sermon we sat through. We heard the call, over and over again: "If you want to be saved by Jesus then you must completely turn your back on sin. If you ever turn to sin again then you are automatically turning your back on Jesus. Make your choice. What will it be: *Jesus* or *sin*?" As far as we could understand, the ultimatum seemed pretty simple: If we kept sinning, we would be lost and with no hope of being saved by Jesus. On the other hand, if we diligently turned away from every sinful act then we could have Jesus and be saved by Him. This is what my naïve crew of friends and I were taught when we were teens, and not surprisingly, this is precisely what we ended up believing. Over time, it became clear this teaching either produces the death of faith due to unbearable *condemnation* or the pursuit of *self-righteousness* through unsustainably energetic moral performance.

SPIRITUAL ZEAL PLUS IGNORANCE EQUALS DISASTER

If we really hadn't authentically cared in the first place and had not been paying attention to what our teachers were saying, then it might have been all right. But for those of us who really cared and genuinely wanted to know the truth, we thought long and hard about the concepts we were hearing. We came to the rational conclusion that we must all morally labor our way to obtain that "difficult prize of salvation." This, we believed, could only be done by getting our lives on track behaviorally. After all, "God hates sin, doesn't He?"

So in our teenage zeal and ignorance, we learned to feel close to God when we had a near-perfect day, and a million miles away from Him when we messed up. We learned to sweat if we weren't having an ultra-committed week regarding the spiritual disciplines of prayer, confession, and Bible reading, but we felt approved by God when we meticulously followed through with these "religious" activities.

MY BLOODY ATTEMPTS AT A GUILT-FREE CONSCIENCE

I remember one event that took place around three months after starting my journey into faith. On this day, I stumbled and committed an act I knew was wrong. I came home to my parents' house that evening and was so overwhelmed by guilt I didn't know what to do. My sixteen-year-old heart felt infinitely distant from God, and the shame I was experiencing was unbearable. All I wanted was to feel reconciled to God again after my failure.

It was late, and my family went to bed, but I went into the guest bedroom of our home and closed the door. I popped a couple of caffeine pills, and told God, "I'm going to repent all night long to show you how incredibly sorry I am." I got down on my knees, began a verbal tirade of confession straight from the heart. My confession transitioned to a physical exhibition of sorrow as I rubbed my knuckles on the carpeting until they bled—all this to prove to God how remorseful I was for what I had done. I had wrongly believed all this would somehow reconcile me to God.

WHAT DOES "DOING A 180°" TURN MEAN?

This is what happens when you teach kids who really want truth and salvation that they must turn from their sin to be acceptable to God. What does it really mean to turn away from all your sin? I was trying to understand how to be saved, and it seemed that people kept telling me I had to stop sinning to be saved. I thought to myself: "Yes—I want to do this! I want to turn from my sin. I want to be saved!" But I could never stop sinning completely, even though I gave it my best shot. The terrifying question welled up within me:

> "How much sin must I turn away from to be saved? From the way it sounds, it seems to be an all-or-nothing type of thing. I can either have sin or Jesus. But I cannot stop sinning completely, so how can I really be sure I'm good enough to get to be saved from my sins and get into heaven when I die?"

When you take salvation-by-grace out of the picture and introduce the concept of *salvation-by-goodness* into the equation, you open wide the door to the visitors of Guilt, Fear, Condemnation, Insecurity, and the rest of this unwholesome gang. You essentially say, "Come on in, guys. Make yourselves at home in my life." These troublemakers make horrible guests! They throw Jesus out of the living room, lock the front door so the Holy Spirit can't get in, and don't allow you to answer the phone when your heavenly Father calls. They absolutely terrorize your life! This is especially true for the genuinely zealous people who really want to know they are good enough to be in right relationship with God.

A GLIMPSE OF FREEDOM

Approximately four years later, I was the lead singer for a touring pop rock band with platinum-bleached silver hair, a couple of piercings around my face, and a whole lot of youthful energy. During this time, I yearned for God and His truth with all my heart—more than anything else in my life. For a moment, the fog cleared and I grasped the true benefits of Jesus' all-sufficient sin-cleansing work on the cross.

It is Jesus' beautiful, fully completed work on the cross that cleanses a person from all sin guilt and makes him holy and blameless before God. Better yet, this forgiveness is given to a person because they believe and receive Jesus as the Savior from their sins—and all this apart from any grading of their shortcomings.

In this time of emotional intimacy with God, song lyrics poured out of me. In this brief moment of clarity, I thought of the whitest, cleanest thing I could envision. I imagined a picture of a graceful, white dove flying in a gentle and pristine snowfall. The image was pure, and the lyrics reflected these thoughts. I called the song, "Dove in a Snowstorm." The lyrics went like this:

DOVE IN THE SNOWSTORM

Cutting myself doesn't do any good…
'cause my blood is as guilty as my hands.
Oh, to replace that past innocence,
to go back to the cradle again —
Oh, to go back to the cradle again.

The rock of my burden, the dirt of my stain —
I can't seem to sweep it away.
The weight of my sin is as heavy as Hell,
so I will put it on this other Man —
I will put it on this other Man.

Now I'm pure…
Like a dove in a snowstorm

Silver means nothing to the one who owns it all,
and gold was not what I needed.
It was His blood that paid the ransom to set my soul free,
God emptied His pockets for me.
God emptied His pockets for me.

Now I'm pure…
Like a dove in a snowstorm

FREEDOM FROM THE HEAVY YOKE

Sadly, the revelation that hit me while I wrote this song didn't stick, and I drifted back into the fog of a faulty, works-oriented understanding of salvation—a salvation confused and lost from my grip once again due to false teaching. The teaching promoting this defective perspective of the Gospel was pervasive, and I found it taught and re-taught in the books and teachings I interacted with.

It wasn't until three or four years later, at the pop rock age of twenty-three, when I came to understand the fullness of all Jesus had accomplished on the cross—and this time I got it for good. What a wonderful thing to finally discover salvation was available apart from all my impossible moral laboring as an utterly free gift for the one who puts his trust in Jesus alone to make him right with God. I immediately spoke with all my friends, asking: "Did you know we are forgiven, made completely right with God, and on our way to heaven because Jesus died for us?" This wonderful new truth was mind-blowing—especially considering the heavy burden I had been carrying for so long. I was never the same again!

A NEW LIFE OF FREEDOM IN JESUS

If anyone wants to do a 180° turn, he should perform a quick spin on his heels, turning away from all attempts to earn salvation by good works and moral behavior. Instead of self-righteousness, let all who desire to be saved turn to a simple trust in Jesus, knowing full well that His finished work on the cross is enough to earn us all we need to be saved, including forgiveness of sins, right standing with God, and an eternal home in heaven.

Jesus was punished for our sins so that we don't have to be. The cross is where we can leave all our sin guilt behind and find true peace with God. Today, I walk in full, unwavering assurance of my salvation—not because of anything I've done, but because of what Jesus did for me. I still make mistakes, but when I do, I know there is no condemnation for those who have placed their trust in Jesus.

With God's help, I will never go back into the slavery of my futile attempts to earn salvation through moral reformation. I pray that you learn from my story, and I encourage you to evaluate your understanding of the Gospel, making sure to fully trust in the Savior who is willing and able to save you completely.

— *Chapter 3* —

HOW TO HAVE YOUR SINS DELETED

WHILE THE BIBLE teaches you *ought to* live a good life, it also makes it clear you can't be made right before God by being a good person. Without a doubt, the God of the Bible is a God of love, full of tender care for the humans He made so wonderfully, and He desires to be with them for eternity. While God's goodness is a highlight in the Scriptures, we must point to sin to assure we have a full picture of reality. It is the full knowledge of a person's sin and guilt before God that assures a person is spiritually "ripe" to receive the Gospel.

Let's analyze this for a minute to gain a deeper understanding. Imagine there is a massive computer sitting up in heaven's courtroom, and a record for every person that has ever lived is stored on this computer. Imagine now a file with *your* name on it. I bet you'd like to know what's in that file, wouldn't you? Okay, I'll let you have a peek, but I'm not so sure you'll like what you see. Within this file exists a list of every single sin you've ever committed, from the cradle to the present, each entry possessing a detailed note of the event to the most meticulous degree.

How exactly does this computer determine which of your actions to categorize as "sin"? Well, this is easy, and it can be done with great precision: *Sin* is determined by using the standard of the written commandments found in the Holy Bible—God's revelation of His will to humanity. Whether in thought or deed, if you ever do anything that goes against any commandments of the biblical Law or the principles associated with them, you become guilty of a sin crime. Yes, your every sin is carefully recorded and stored in your file to stand as a witness against you on judgment day. Scary thought, huh?

Although there may not be an actual computer in heaven, our imagination game was not that far away from reality. The Bible tells us every sin we commit *is* actually recorded in the books of heaven, ready to be brought forward on our future court date. Here we read a description:

> Then I saw a great white throne and Him who was seated on it. The earth and the heavens fled from His presence, and there was no place for them. And I saw the dead, great and small, standing before the throne, and books were opened. Another book was opened, which is the book of life. The dead were judged according to what they had done as recorded in the books.
> Revelation 20:11–12, NIV

There you have it: Your evil deeds are written in a book, and someday, if you cannot figure out a way to clear your record, you'll be judged for everything recorded there. Tough deal! So what exactly is written in your book?

ADDING SIN IS EASY; SUBTRACTING SIN IS QUITE ANOTHER THING

Interestingly enough, it's extraordinarily easy to *add* to our criminal record in heaven, isn't it? All you have to do is break a rule through something evil you do or think (a sin of *commission*), or through something good you fail to do (a sin of *omission*). Unfortunately, the tricky thing is trying to figure out how to get these sin-crimes off our records once they are there. With a careful look at this situation, we must reasonably conclude that with each year that passes us by, the lists of crimes on our records naturally get longer and longer. It also makes sense to conclude that our lists of sin-crimes never get shorter—not even during the best years of our lives.

Some people are convinced if they compensate for their past sins by doing lots of good things and promising never to sin again, God will let them off the hook. But does this way of thinking really make sense? Let me ask you a question: If you got caught speeding and were slammed with a hefty speeding ticket, would helping an old lady cross the road cause your ticket to disappear? What if you promised to do ten good things to make up for your single act of breaking the speed limit? What if you swore on your great-grandmother's grave that you'd never speed again? Would any of these things cause the legal system to drop your ticket? No, of course, they wouldn't. Not even a chance. Similarly, it is laughable for anyone to think their good deeds or abstinence from bad deeds could delete any of their sin-crimes that have already hit heaven's books.

WHAT IS THE STANDARD?

Every human being will one day stand before the judgment seat of God. The Bible says: "… [E]ach person is destined to die once and after that comes judgment…" (Hebrews 9:27, NLT) If sin doesn't go away no matter what we do, what then is the standard we must live up to if we want to be "saved" on judgment day when we settle accounts with God? I'm glad you asked. Actually, the Holy Bible has something distressing to say on this topic. It teaches us:

> For the person who keeps all the laws except one is as guilty as a person who has broken all of God's laws.
> James 2:10, NLT

Tough deal! From what we just read, the God of the Universe is not the kind of judge who weighs sin on a balance, acquitting those whose good outweighs their evil. Instead, according to the Bible verse above, He is the kind of judge who demands *absolute moral perfection.*

Adam and Eve experienced the inflexibility of God's perfect standard. Do you remember what happened in Eden? Adam and Eve were banished from God's presence upon their first "slip-up." All this leads us to a harsh realization: One sin or many, any negative entry on our sin records becomes an insurmountable obstacle between God and us. Yes, one sin is enough to earn a person the "sinner" label, and is enough to damn a person when they stand before God. The Bible declares: "For everyone has sinned; we all fall short of God's glorious standard" (Romans 3:23, NLT).

ONE SIN PER DAY?

It absolutely amazes me that we imagine it possible to make ourselves right in God's eyes by obeying His commandments. Don't we see how incredibly far we are from being good enough? Just for fun, let's say there exists a genuine "straight A" type of lady—someone out there who is an exceptionally good person. Let's say this girl is so morally conscientious that she only committed one sin per day. When compared with her peers, one sin per day would certainly place her in the top 1 percent for her fine performance. This person is truly the moral "cream of the crop." Yet how does the Judge of heaven look at this situation? What is His perspective? If our lady only sinned once per day—which is an outstanding performance for any human being—she would find her sin record would be hundreds of pages long by the end of her life. In fact, if she sinned only once per day from age five to eighty-five, she would have 29,200 sin-crimes on her record on the day she died! But as we have already determined, *quantity* is really not the issue. Why? Because one sin on a person's record is enough to damn a person on judgment day.

IT'S ALL A PART OF GOD'S MASTER PLAN

If God knew we couldn't perfectly follow His Law with all its written commandments, why did He give them to us in the first place? Again, the Apostle Paul perfectly dealt with this thoughtful question in the following:

> Obviously, the law applies to those to whom it was given, for its purpose is to keep people from having excuses, and to show that the entire world is guilty before God. For no one

can ever be made right with God by doing what the law commands. The law simply shows us how sinful we are.
Romans 3:19–20, NLT

So God gave the written commandments so that we could see how we've failed His standard. The Law gives us an awareness of our sins through God's eyes. We have all sinned against God's ways from our earliest years, and only when we analyze the written Law do we realize how morally depraved we are. The Law is a lot like a mirror, showing us where we have food on our face, where our hair is messed up, what we've missed in our shave, or where our makeup has been smeared. We wouldn't see our physical flaws if we didn't have a mirror. In the same way, God's law shows us where we are out of place. Out of love, God gave us the written Law to help us see our sin, admit our guilt, and come to Him for help.

ONLY ONE WAY OUT

So how can we be made right with God by having our many sins completely deleted? Is it possible? Well, when there was absolutely no way of saving ourselves from the condemnation and punishment awaiting us on judgment day, Jesus stepped in and took the situation into His hands. We had utterly failed to live up to God's standard of perfection, but Jesus lived a morally and legally perfect life, flawlessly satisfying God's standard. When we couldn't do a single thing to remove the sin-crimes from our heavenly sin records, it was almost as if Jesus jumped in and said:

> "Heavenly Father, here I am. I have done nothing wrong and deserve no punishment of My own, but I will take on the punishment for their sins. Punish Me fully for every sin-

crime that they've ever committed, and then remove those sin-crimes from their records forever. I will take the cross for them."

This is amazing news—especially if you have dishonored God by sinning at any point in your life. If you will wholeheartedly believe Jesus took the punishment for you, God has promised to take His index finger and press the "delete" button on heaven's computer, clearing your sin record forever. How can a person have their sins deleted? It is only through faith in Jesus and His finished work on the cross that a person can be pardoned from sins. This is what the God of justice and love desired all along!

A WORD TO KNOW: JUSTIFIED

Someone once said the word *justified* means "just as if I'd never sinned." It is true! In the original language of the Scriptures, this word was a legal term. When a person is "justified," they are declared "innocent" in the eyes of the court system. The same thing applies when we place our faith in Jesus. We are *justified* the instant we put our full trust in Jesus' sacrificial work to save us from our sins and make us right with God. God sees our faith in Jesus—the Savior who died on the cross for our sins—and He declares us "justified." Now it is just as if we'd never sinned!

Part 2

SELF-RIGHTEOUSNESS: A SERIAL KILLER IN A SUIT AND TIE

— *Chapter 4* —

THE TROJAN HORSE GOSPEL

*I marvel that you are turning away so soon from Him
who called you in the grace of Christ, to a different gospel,
which is not another; but there are some who trouble
you and want to pervert the Gospel of Christ.*
Galatians 1:6–7, NKJV

I F THEY COULD not succeed by might, they would win by deceit. As the ancient story goes, the Greeks were unsuccessful in their ten-year siege of the large and prosperous city of Troy. Utterly frustrated by the impenetrable walls, but refusing to give up the assault, they developed a crafty, one-of-a-kind plot that would go down in history. The Greeks constructed a giant victory trophy for their opponents—a colossal wooden statue of a horse—and wheeled it up to the city gates and left it there. Getting in their boats and sailing out of sight, it appeared that the Greeks forfeited the fight and returned to homeland across the sea. The people of the city cheered in celebration at their triumph, and opened the gates to wheel the massive wooden horse into the safety of their massive city walls. This iconic statue, they believed, would stand as a monument of their great success for many years to come. However, what started out as a joyous victory party ended in stunning defeat. In the middle of the night, while the people of the city were sleeping, a hidden trap door opened on the underbelly of the giant wooden horse, and out climbed an elite group of Greek warriors that had been hiding within. These killers were smuggled through the city's gates inside the trusted Trojan horse. Once out of their wooden hiding place, these assassins crept their way through the streets of Troy, lurking in the shadows, making their way to the city gates. They overcame the guards at the city entrance, and opened wide the front gates of Troy to the Greek army that had returned in the cover of night. The Greeks flooded in and captured the city, and this is how the invincible city of Troy fell.

A SPIRITUAL TROJAN HORSE

The God of the universe has shown His great love for humanity by providing a way for us to be forgiven of our sins. He did this so that we could be free from condemnation and spend eternity by His side. When a person puts their full faith in the Savior, Jesus, the walls of salvation are immediately erected around him or her.

From this point forward, this believer is protected from the enemy's assaults against the wall that come through accusation, guilt, and the threats of separation from God and condemnation in hell. The believer, seeing the indestructible fortification walls surrounding, may yell back through the gate: "Yes, devil, I still make mistakes. I know I deserve punishment for my sins. But Jesus loved me and took the punishment I deserved when He died in my place. Accuse me all you want, but your accusations will not break through these walls of salvation built by Jesus Himself." The believer is secure in this spiritual safe haven, and the accuser stands outside with no power to get in. This safety persists as long as the believer trusts in these great walls *and lets nothing else in.*

This is where our frustrated enemy must change his tactic. His strategy for getting to us looks suspiciously like the trickery of the Trojan Horse. The true Gospel cannot be defeated by all the force the devil can muster, but as the Bible so frequently warns us, false concepts can be added to the true Gospel—like soldiers in the belly of the wooden horse. When this occurs, all that once made sense about God's plan for salvation becomes infiltrated by irrationality. In the end, the Gospel gets so twisted that it ceases to have the power to save.

THE REAL DEAL

The Bible teaches a Gospel that puts all the attention on Jesus and instructs us to rely on Him alone for forgiveness of sins, right standing with God, and citizenship in heaven. It speaks of spiritual salvation as being a gift given to all who believe Jesus took the punishment for their sins when He died in their place. It is simple. It is pure. It is biblical. It is Gospel. This lines up well with what the Bible has to say:

> For God so loved the world that He gave His one and only Son, that whoever believes in Him shall not perish but have eternal life. For God did not send His Son into the world to condemn the world, but to save the world through Him. Whoever believes in Him is not condemned, but whoever does not believe stands condemned already because they have not believed in the name of God's one and only Son.
> John 3:16–18, NIV

Notice the focus is on Jesus. This passage makes it clear that the person who wants to be saved needs only to believe in Jesus and he receives the blessings of salvation. If he believes, there will be no condemnation for sin, and he will inherit eternal life with God in heaven. That's it. That's the Gospel, and it gives no attention to us at all but focuses all the glory and praise on the Savior alone. The following is a simple example of a presentation of the Gospel as the Bible teaches it:

> "We deserved to be punished for our sins and separated from God, but Jesus took upon Himself our guilt and all the punishment we deserved when He died on the cross in our place. We must trust in Jesus and His sacrificial work as that thing that earns us our forgiveness and right standing with God. If we put our faith in Him alone for our salvation, we receive forgiveness, reconciliation with God, and an eternal place in heaven."

Again, notice all the attention has been placed on Jesus, and the only requirement for salvation is to trust in Him to save us.

A LOOK INSIDE THE BELLY OF THE HORSE

The devil likes to use religious lingo to cloak his lies in a disguise that seems trustworthy. Because the language used seems so harmless on the surface, many unknowingly accept the false gospel through the gates of their minds. Now let's look into the belly of the devil's Trojan Horse gospel and see what is concealed within. While the true Gospel focuses on Jesus and how He alone can make us legally righteous in God's eyes, the assassins hiding within the false gospel strike at us with concepts of *self-righteousness*. A false gospel turns the attention back on us—on our performance—how good or bad we perform for God in our daily lives. A way to identify a false gospel is to note any teaching that talks about Jesus and then adds "*and*" or "*but*" to it. The following are two examples of the many forms a false gospel can take:

- **THE *AND* GOSPEL**: "Friend, salvation is through faith in Jesus alone. It's all about Him and His grace. If you believe in Jesus *and* turn from your sins you will be saved."
- **THE *BUT* GOSPEL**: "Yes, Jesus died for our sins. We must put our faith in Him *but* we must also turn from our sins if we want to be saved."

These statements are Trojan Horse imposters and the deadly assassins of self-righteousness are lurking all throughout.

A DEEPER LOOK

It is common for false gospels to throw people off by beginning with a declaration that faith in Jesus is the way to salvation and that works have nothing to do with it. This is not at all what is meant, but it is stated to bring down the guards of the listeners. The true intention comes out shortly after as the bait-and-switch occurs. If you watch carefully, the innocent-sounding beginning gets contradicted by a statement which demands that people "believe in Jesus *and* turn from your sins" to be saved. This reveals the true, self-righteous nature of the message being presented. (Note: While it is good for believers to turn from their sins, it is spiritual suicide to believe this activity helps save us in any way) Remember, forgiveness of sins occurs because of what Jesus has done, not anything we have done. The emphasis is on the cross, not our works.

We have now opened the trap door under the horse and watched the assassins of self-righteousness fall to the ground. We see the Trojan Horse gospel for what it is. A false gospel presentation firmly puts the focus of our attention onto our day-to-day performance, suggesting that if we want to be worthy of God's salvation, we must work to clean up our act. If allowed access into our lives, these assassins would destroy our assurance of salvation and reliance on the Savior, eventually tearing down the walls of our salvation from the inside out. Shortly after these assassins get in, we ask the following questions:

- "I believe in Jesus, but am I good enough to be saved?"
- "I believe in Jesus, but have I sinned too much lately? Would I go to heaven if I died today?"
- "I sin almost every day, and knowing all sins are equally as grievous to God, does my faith in Jesus really overcome my guilt?"

The nature of these questions makes it clear the person asking them does not trust in Jesus alone for their salvation as the lack of assurance makes this reality evident. The results for people who fall for these assassins of self-righteousness will be that (a) they believe they are good enough to be saved, or (b) they believe they can't live good enough to be saved. Both options are just as perilous. Many others who let these assassins through their gates will be too lazy to really analyze the situation and will one day pass into eternity without being sure where they are going.

THE SAFE WALLS OF SALVATION

So here is the lesson to be learned from the story of the Trojan Horse: Trust in the Savior who can fully save you, and be watchful for the traps the enemy of your soul sets for you. Avoid his traps—especially the one set to extinguish the most important message of all. When listening to someone teach on the Gospel, pay less attention to the spiritual-sounding words being used and more attention to the *concepts* being taught. Does the message you are hearing teach that our salvation is bought and paid for by Jesus and that simple faith in Him is enough to save you? If so, great! Let the speaker of those words be blessed! This is the biblical, God-engineered path to salvation for human beings who can never reach God's standard of perfection on their own. On the other hand, does the "gospel" message you are hearing start out with words like "grace" and "faith" but then contradict itself by adding an "and" or "but," saying that you have to behave your way to salvation? If so, then you have just stumbled on a bona fide Trojan Horse. Lock your gates and don't think twice.

Remember, we could never behave or reform our way to right standing with God, and this is precisely why Jesus had to come and die in the first place. Realizing our inability to save ourselves, He took upon Himself the full punishment due us for our many sins, and because he has paid our penalty in full, we are freed from guilt, condemnation, and punishment. Our sin records are completely pardoned by God through our faith in Jesus. This is truly a gift from beginning to end. Let this be both a warning and encouragement to always stay safely within the mighty walls of the Salvation.

A WORD TO KNOW: LAW

Biblically, the word "Law" most often refers to God's written commandments as found in the Bible—especially those laws recorded in the first five books of the Bible. A famous Rabbi once counted all the individual commandments of God written in the first five books of the Bible alone and determined that there were 613 laws. Each of God's commandments is healthy for society, and by obeying them we are actually showing love toward mankind and love toward God. God's law shows us how to distinguish right from wrong, and it teaches us what perfection is and what it is not. Most importantly, God's law shows us our need for forgiveness and propels us toward the Savior. The word "Law" is referred to 223 times in the New Testament.

Chapter 5

THE REPENTANCE MASQUERADE

*Yet we know that a person is made right with God by faith
in Jesus Christ, not by obeying the law. And we have believed in
Christ Jesus, so that we might be made right with God because of
our faith in Christ, not because we have obeyed the law. For no
one will ever be made right with God by obeying the law.*
Galatians 2:16, NLT

O NE NIGHT MY wife and I felt like having a night on the town, so we threw on costumes and went out to a masquerade ball. We arrived at the event, slipped on our masks, and headed into the massive master ballroom where the lively event was taking place. We gazed across a sea of a thousand faces all tightly packed together, each one hidden behind an extraordinarily creative disguise. At one point, I left my wife alone for a few minutes to grab some refreshments. Shortly after that, I returned to the general vicinity where I had last seen my wife. Scanning through the masks, I found the one I was looking for and handed her a beverage and a plate of her favorite appetizers. Unfortunately, an unfamiliar voice behind the mask responded: "I have a feeling you've got the wrong Joker mask here. But thanks anyway." I laughed and walked away. Just an instant of interaction with the person behind the mask helped me realize I had found the *right* mask but the *wrong* person. As I hacked my way through the forest of people, someone tapped me on the shoulder. I spun around and saw another Joker mask, but this time a familiar voice asked, "Where were you? I thought you got eaten by the tiger."

A LANGUAGE MIX-UP

As fun as the previous story was, it never happened. The story was fashioned to help us illustrate another serious misunderstanding that has been taking place, but this time the mix-up is taking place in the realm of language—a mix-up that has serious consequences in our understanding of the Gospel. The confusion is over the word *repent*.

The word *repent* can be found in two popular and important salvation verses in the New Testament, yet we find people today attributing different meanings to this word. Some say it means one thing, and others say it means something else. As in our masquerade illustration, sometimes things can look the same on the surface but what's hidden behind can be drastically different. What we need to do is find out which definition God originally intended.

THE TWO MOST MISINTERPRETED PASSAGES IN THE BIBLE

Acts 2:28 and Acts 3:19 are the two New Testament passages where the word *repent* plays a key role in a Gospel presentation, and interesting enough, these are the two most misinterpreted passages in the entire Bible. As we read these verses, we find the apostle Peter speaking to a group of religious Jews in Jerusalem only fifty days after Jesus' crucifixion, burial, and bodily resurrection. In fact, it had only been ten days since Jesus had left His disciples and ascended into heaven. With this said, Jesus was fresh on the minds of the people of this city. Jerusalem was overflowing with people and bustling with visitors from around the world because it was the day of a prominent religious holiday (called *Shavuot* in Hebrew language and *Pentecost* in the Greek language). In our two focal passages of Acts 2:28 and Acts 3:19, Peter addresses some people who had recently rejected Jesus, failing to recognize He was the Savior and Messiah God had sent their way. Upon hearing Peter's message, the crowd was deeply moved, and asked: "Brothers, what should we do?" Peter responded:

> Repent and be baptized, every one of you, in the name of Jesus Christ for the forgiveness of your sins. And you will receive the gift of the Holy Spirit.
> Acts 2:38, NIV

In his next speech Peter continued to urge the people of Jerusalem:

> Repent, then, and turn to God, so that your sins may be wiped out, that times of refreshing may come from the Lord.
> Acts 3:19, NIV

THE WRONG DEFINITION

Now that we've read these two popular verses, let's talk about the confusion that arises from this tricky word. The problem lies in the fact that some people wrongly define the word *repent* as "to turn away from all your sins." When used this way in the context of the Gospel, it doesn't take a rocket scientist to figure out that this definition will produce great confusion. Let's reread these two passages, but plug in the faulty definition of *repent* and see what happens:

> [Turn away from all your sins] and be baptized, every one of you, in the name of Jesus Christ for the forgiveness of your sins. And you will receive the gift of the Holy Spirit.
> Acts 2:38, NIV

> [Turn away from all your sins], then, and turn to God, so that your sins may be wiped out, that times of refreshing may come from the Lord.
> Acts 3:19, NIV

If a person did not know any better, they might listen to the wrong definition of the word *repent*, read these Gospel verses, and come out completely confused on the other side. This has happened many times. Even sincere people fall for this trap, and they end up thinking:

> "I'm confused! Someone told me that repent means 'to turn away from all your sins.' This means the apostle Peter taught we must turn away from all our sins—repent—to receive forgiveness of sins. But I thought all I needed to do was place my faith in Jesus and His work on the cross to be saved. Which way is it? Is Jesus enough, or do I also have to clean up my act to *gain* and *maintain* salvation?"

The previous quotation brings up some great rational questions—questions that must be answered. The Bible is God's Word, and it never contradicts itself, so we can rest assured the true biblical perspective will make complete sense.

UNMASKING THE COUNTERFEIT

This apparent contradiction is really no contradiction at all. We can attribute all the confusion to a wrong, unbiblical definition attached to the word *repent*. All people who attempt to purify themselves enough for God are trying to ride their rocking horses up Mount Everest. All who attempt to become right with God by piling up good works are only building a Tower of Babel that will never reach heaven. The self-reformation "gospel" will never lead a person to right standing with God, and many religious people will find a sad surprise when they finally get to heaven's gates only to be refused entrance. Then they will realize they had been duped out of their unadulterated faith in Jesus by a lie that came to them in religious-sounding lingo. Paul saw the danger behind the mask and warned:

> For if you are trying to make yourselves right with God by keeping the law, you have been cut off from Christ! You have fallen away from God's grace.
> Galatians 5:4, NLT

Paul *was not* telling us we shouldn't abide by God's moral Law; in fact, Paul always urged believers to obey God and live righteous lives. However, he *was* warning us we should never place even an ounce of trust in our behavioral performance to make us right with God. If we do, we inescapably cut ourselves off from Jesus and fall away from God's grace. Listen to this warning and check your heart. Have you trusted in your behavioral performance in any way to earn right standing with God?

THE TRUE DEFINITION OF "REPENT"

Fortunately, there is a solution to the tension regarding the definition of the word *repent*. As we mentioned earlier, there are two ways people define the word *repent* in the context of salvation. One definition is accurate and in full alignment with God's original intention; the other is destructively false. The two definitions of the word *repent* are:

- **INCORRECT DEFINITION:** *To turn away from all your sins.*
- **CORRECT DEFINITION:** *To change your mind about something.*

To put it plainly, the first definition is altogether unfaithful to the original Greek language in which the New Testament was written. On the other hand, the second definition faithfully defines the word *repent* we find in the New Testament. The Greek word used in the original manuscripts of the Bible was the imperative word *metanoēsate* in the second person plural, and Bible translators interpreted this word into English by using the word *repent*. To break it down, the original Greek foundation word—*metanoeō*—comes from the following root words: *meta* ("after") and *noeō* ("to think upon"). A correct biblical understanding of this Greek word is: "To change your mind."[2]

Now let's reread our two passages from the book of Acts, but this time we will plug in the correct definition of *repent* and see what happens. In perfect alignment with the context of these two passages, Peter was urging the people of Jerusalem to *change their*

---

[2] "G3340 - metanoéō - Strong's Greek Lexicon (KJV)." Blue Letter Bible, www.blueletterbible.org//lang/lexicon/lexicon.cfm?Strongs=G3340&t=KJV

minds about their unbelief in Jesus, and instead, think differently by trusting He was the Messiah who came to save them from their sins.

> [Change your mind] and be baptized, every one of you, in the name of Jesus Christ for the forgiveness of your sins. And you will receive the gift of the Holy Spirit.
> (Acts 2:38)

> [Change your mind], then, and turn to God, so that your sins may be wiped out, that times of refreshing may come from the Lord.
> (Acts 3:19)

It is so important that I will say it again: In the context of Acts 2:38 and Acts 3:19, Peter was urging his listeners to change their minds (repent) from unbelief in Jesus to full faith in Him as their Savior. Peter said if they did this, they would receive forgiveness for their sins. This was the repentance Peter was referring to, and it is the kind that upholds the true Gospel, putting all focus for our salvation on Jesus and His finished work on the cross.

THE DIRE TREND: "REPENT AND BELIEVE"

Today, the devil has made his inroads into the church's "gospel" presentations, and it breaks my heart. In many, many sermons, books, audio recordings, and videos, we hear the call to "repent and believe." This would be perfectly fine if only the word *repent* were used in the manner the Gospel verses use it. Sadly, often it is not. As we accept the devil's definition for "repent"—the definition of "to turn from sin"—we allow works and moral reformation to become a prerequisite for salvation. The term "repent and believe" then wrongly becomes a call with *two* distinct and contradictory features:

1. Turn from your sin (stop sinning)
2. Believe in Jesus as Savior

The common call to "repent and believe" to obtain salvation includes two *contradictory* requirements—and the devil knows it. You cannot trust that your salvation is owed solely to what Jesus did for you while also believing your self-reformation saves you. Said another way, you can't trust Jesus as the one who saves you if He doesn't save you fully. Any salvation call to "repent and believe" that defines "repent" as turning from sin is ultimately teaching a works-based "gospel" message—a false "gospel." There is nothing good about this so-called "good news."

People will push back against what was just said. They will bring misguided accusations, saying that any "gospel" that doesn't include turning from sin encourages a loose and wild lifestyle of debauchery—a license to sin. Virtually every time I have stood in front of a crowd to bring the Jesus-focused Gospel message to encourage a refutation of self-righteousness, someone will come up afterward to chastise me. They will say, "Yes, Beau, it is certainly salvation by faith alone. But if you don't put a requirement to turn away from sin, people will keep on sinning." I respond,

> "I believe salvation is by faith alone, and I have no additional baggage to add. This is the Gospel. You might be surprised to know my view of the Gospel has done nothing but fill me with the desire to turn from my sin out of gratitude for the gift of salvation I have received. But I will never trust in my good works or turning from sin to play any part in my salvation—not even 1 percent. I trust in

Jesus to make me right with God, and the Bible adds nothing else to this Gospel equation—and I won't either."

A WORD TO KNOW: REPENT

The word "repent" does NOT mean "to turn from all your sins." Instead, the true original word that the New Testament used was the Greek word *metanoēsate*. *Metanoēsate* means to "change your mind" about something, and it does NOT mean to "turn from all your sins." When people in the New Testament were talking about being saved, they would use the word *metanoēsate* to urge people to "change their minds" from unbelief in Jesus to full faith in Him. It is by this faith in Jesus that God would forgive the believer of their sins and save them. After Jesus died on the cross and resurrected, unbelievers are called to "repent" by *changing their minds* from unbelief to belief in the Savior.

Chapter 6

WHEN THE HOOK OF LAW IS FOUND HIDDEN WITHIN GRACE

F JESUS TOOK the full punishment for our sins when He gave His life, why we would need to fear God's judgment or condemnation anymore? If we have Jesus as our Savior, why then should we listen to accusations from the devil and men when they tell us we aren't good enough for God? Of course, we're not good enough for God—of this we are certain! However, Jesus *was* good enough for God, and when we put our faith in Him as our Savior, He makes us right with God. This right standing with God does not come through making our outward behavior perfect, but by making our sin records perfect. He bore our punishment, and then He deleted every record of crime associated with our names. With knowledge of these truths, the enemy's accusatory ammo has no power over us. We wear the bulletproof vests of the knowledge of our perfect righteousness attained through the Savior.

HOW THE DEVIL USES RELIGIOUS-SOUNDING LANGUAGE TO DECEIVE

Let us identify how the devil and false teachers use religious-sounding language to trick us out of fully trusting Jesus for our salvation. The following is an example of a false teaching we often see. It is important for each of us to skillfully identify it. You will certainly notice many spiritual words sprinkled throughout; hopefully, you will also notice the several virtuous portions of teaching included. But the most important thing for the fish to notice about bait is not the worm, but the *hook*. Now read the following paragraph carefully:

> We believe that salvation is an act of God's grace that is accessed through faith in Jesus Christ. No person can be good enough to earn salvation, and 'being good' does not contribute to receiving God's love and favor (Ephesians 2:8, 13). We believe that, when people repent for their sins and accept Christ, they are justified through Jesus' sacrificial death on the cross. To repent means to be sorry for sins, but it also means to turn away from a sinful lifestyle. Accepting Christ means believing in Him as the only Savior (Romans 10:9–10; 1 John 1:9).

We can analyze the previous quotation by acknowledging some worthy concepts included. However, a pinch of poison sprinkled over a table full of food makes a deadly meal. Let's think about it. First, we see the quoted statement of beliefs tells us no person can be good enough to earn salvation and "being good" does *not* contribute to receiving God's love and favor. Excellent! This is absolutely true according to the Scriptures. Second, it then transitions to say Jesus can only save a person if they first "turn away from a sinful lifestyle." This is where the train jumps off the track. The second statement contradicts the first. It first says you cannot be saved by "being good," yet in the next breath, it declares you must make yourself *good enough* by turning away from all your sins. This sounds a lot like the slick car salesman who announces: "Friend, I have a gift for you. It will only cost you ten dollars" With that said, let's now try this again with another statement of belief:

> We are saved by grace—undeserved and unearned—through faith in Jesus Christ, His death, burial, and resurrection. Salvation is a gift of God, not a result of our good works. Because Jesus Christ lived a sinless life, His blood shed on the cross of Calvary is sufficient to cleanse us of sin when appropriated individually through repentance and faith. Jesus allowed Himself to be punished for our sin, enabling all who believe to be free from the penalty of sin. Repentance is a commitment to turn away from sin in every area of our lives and to follow Christ. Through repentance, we individually receive salvation and forgiveness of sin.

How did this one look? According to this statement of belief, are we saved by (a) "a gift of God, not a result of our good works," or (b) by our commitment to be good enough to "turn away from sin in every area of our lives?" This reminds me of the car salesman. I hear a voice saying: "Friend, salvation is a free gift from God, and you really don't have to be 'good enough' to be saved. All you have to do is be 'good enough' to be saved by this gift"?

Caution: Read no further unless you truly understand and have caught the problem red-handed. Go back and re-read this section if you did not fully catch it. You will most certainly need this skill in the real world because this is the devil's favorite trick and his only hope to trap those who love God and His Scriptures.

ANALYSIS

The biggest deception in our faith communities is the fallacy that people can trust in both Jesus and the works of their "repentance" and still be saved. This dueling-focus confusion annuls true faith in the Savior. It sounds so close to the truth, yet it is still so far away.

The Bible teaches we are saved by trusting Jesus to take away our guilt and to make us right with God, and we are to trust in Him *exclusively*. The devil is acutely aware that if he can get a person to believe salvation is conditional and she must turn away from evil and do good to be saved, he has successfully redirected her faith away from the Savior and onto herself. This person is deceived into believing she can help make herself good enough for God—that she must reach the heights of some unknown standard of obedience before receiving the gift of salvation. It is as if salvation were some ancient Greek mountaintop where God stood—a mountain that Olympians must ascend in their strength to receive the golden crown as a prize. This is not the metaphor for salvation that the Bible teaches.

Salvation has been and always will be a gift given by a perfect God to imperfect sinners. You must not try to ascend mountains or work yourself into shape before approaching God. He loves you as you are, and He knows His standard is far beyond any bar you could ever reach. He wants to give you the gift of salvation, but He is offended by all who try to take His gift with the thought in their hearts that they have earned it. He will not give His gift that way.

Yet we know that a person is made right with God by faith
in Jesus Christ, not by obeying the law. And we have believed in
Christ Jesus, so that we might be made right with God because of
our faith in Christ, not because we have obeyed the law. For no
one will ever be made right with God by obeying the law.
Galatians 2:16, NLT

A WORD TO KNOW: SELF-RIGHTEOUSNESS

The word *"self-righteousness"* means *believing your behavior is good enough to achieve or play a part in achieving your salvation.* In the context of the biblical Gospel, this word has bad connotations. Self-righteousness is a belief that makes saving faith in Jesus impossible because saving faith requires full faith that Jesus alone can save us. Self-righteousness believes our efforts help save us, and this means the self-righteous person does not fully trust in Jesus to save him or her. People who struggle with self-righteousness cannot be saved by Jesus until they give up their self-righteousness.

— *Chapter 7* —

5 STATEMENTS OF BELIEF BEGGING FOR EVALUATION

AT THIS POINT, do you feel you can easily discern the true Gospel from its counterfeits with no confusion? Can you identify when the simple, biblical Gospel is being twisted to move away from the metaphor of sacrifice (the innocent taking the punishment for the guilty)? Remember, Jesus' finished work on the cross is the beginning and end of God's salvation message, and the equation is *Jesus + Nothing = Salvation*. Believers do not add any other requirements for the gift of salvation but simple faith in what Jesus did for us on the cross.

This book has been carefully engineered to help you understand the "science of salvation," teaching you to split the very hairs of each biblical and unbiblical concept with absolute precision, discerning truth from fallacy. Why? So you will avoid the pitfalls and snares the devil has laid for you, escape the condemnation to hell, and safely make it to heaven. This book will help you learn how to stand firm for the truth and to position yourself courageously against nearly every distortion of the Gospel that's lurking around out there.

THE 5 STATEMENTS OF BELIEF

Now here is a chance to test your Gospel discernment skills. The following five statements of belief were among the first ten available in search engine results for churches in New York City. They have not been altered or edited in any way; what you see is what was posted on the church websites.

Can you effectively assess the following five statements of belief? When it comes down to it, discerning the truthfulness or error in doctrinal statements is ultimately where the rubber meets the road for the believer. If you can accurately point out both the good and the bad in these five so-called "gospel" presentations, then you probably can (a) be certain of your salvation, (b) defend the Gospel from false teachers, and (c) communicate the salvation message with others who need to hear it.

In the following, you will see five examples of statements of beliefs regarding how a person can obtain salvation. See if you can identify which of the following three categories you feel each statement falls into, including:

- **BIBLICAL:** Aligns with the Gospel as the Bible describes it.
- **UNBIBLICAL:** Does not align with the Gospel we see in Bible.
- **UNDECIDED:** You are not sure for one reason or another.

I urge you to read each statement well enough to make a final judgment. As you read each statement of belief, move slowly through each sentence, thinking carefully about what is being said. I will warn you: some statements teach astonishingly *false* information—"gospel" presentations that are a million miles away from the truth. I will also say you will need to be watchful as you proceed because some of these lies are cloaked in religious-sounding lingo. As religious as they may sound, some will certainly lead people away from salvation if believed. Finally, you will see the word "repent" used in some doctrinal statements, so make sure to figure out how this word is being defined. In the end, you are out to determine whether these statements of belief point to Jesus' finished work on the cross for our salvation or wrongly put the spotlight on our moral performance.

Here you go. Let the mental sparks fly.

ALLEGED "GOSPEL" PRESENTATION #1

"SALVATION: We are saved by grace through faith in Jesus Christ; His death, burial, and resurrection. Salvation is a gift from God, not a result of our good works or any human efforts (Ephesians 2:8–9; Galatians 2:16, 3:8; Titus 3:5; Romans 10:9–10; Acts 16:31; Hebrews 9:22).

REPENTANCE: Repentance is the commitment to turn away from sin in every area of our lives and to follow Christ, which allows us to receive His redemption and to be regenerated by the Holy Spirit. Thus, through repentance, we receive forgiveness of sins and appropriate salvation (Acts 2:21, 3:19; 1 John 1:9)."

AUTHOR'S ASSESSMENT OF #1: <u>UNBIBLICAL</u>

As is a common trick of the devil, the first paragraph teaches salvation is only a result of faith, and "not a result of our good works or any human efforts." This disarms the reader and makes him or her feel safe. Then in the second paragraph on repentance, everything in the first paragraph is contradicted. Without a doubt, the second paragraph puts the requirement of human efforts back on the human. This false teaching annuls saving faith in Jesus and we should avoided it at all cost.

ALLEGED "GOSPEL" PRESENTATION #2:

"Are you ready to decide to follow Christ? The only way to find forgiveness from God and begin a relationship with Him is to trust in Jesus' sacrifice for you and repent—turn from your sins. We urge you to take this step of faith today. To do that, simply talk to God—this is called praying—and tell Him you believe in His Son."

AUTHOR'S ASSESSMENT OF #2: <u>UNBIBLICAL</u>

This so-called "gospel" presentation couldn't be further from the truth. It tells the reader that the only way to be forgiven for our sins is to do something completely impossible: be saved by trusting in Jesus' sacrifice to save you, and also trust in your self-reformation (turning from sins) to save you. This is the same ancient deception the devil has been using for two thousand years. By trusting that our self-cleansing helps us to be forgiven and be right with God, it becomes impossible to fully trust in the true Savior for our salvation. Partial faith in Jesus is not saving faith.

ALLEGED "GOSPEL" PRESENTATION #3

"What is this thing we're talking about when we reference 'the gospel?'

The gospel is the good news that while we were once separated from God by our sin, God has provided a way of salvation through the gift of his son Jesus Christ. He suffered as a sacrifice for sin, conquered death through his physical resurrection, and offers salvation to all who will accept it.

The Gospel is unconditional acceptance given to an undeserving person by an unobligated giver."

AUTHOR'S ASSESSMENT OF #3: <u>BIBLICAL</u>

This is a strong Gospel presentation. It effectively explains that humans are separated from God, and it tells readers that Jesus took the punishment for our sins in our place and then resurrected from the dead. This Gospel presentation makes it clear that salvation is a gift to be received by sinners with no conditions other than accepting this gift.

ALLEGED "GOSPEL" PRESENTATION #4

"We believe in salvation through faith in Jesus Christ.
John 3:16, Acts 2:21, Romans 10:9"

AUTHOR'S ASSESSMENT OF #4: <u>BIBLICAL</u> OR <u>UNDECIDED</u>

This Gospel presentation puts the attention on Jesus, rightly telling readers they can be saved by putting their faith in Him. This was meant to be brief, and this is fine. However, a full Gospel presentation would include details about what exactly it is about Jesus we should have faith in. Specifically, a person should have faith that Jesus died on the cross to take the punishment in place of sinners so they would not have to be punished. We want to be specific about what we are trusting in for our salvation.

ALLEGED "GOSPEL" PRESENTATION #5

"Justification by God's grace to all who repent and put their faith in Jesus Christ alone for salvation."

AUTHOR'S ASSESSMENT OF #5: UNBIBLICAL OR UNDECIDED

Justification refers to how God takes away the guilt of sinners, and this presentation tells readers that they must do two things to be saved from their sins: (a) repent, and (b) believe in Jesus Christ alone for salvation.

If the writer of this presentation used the word "repent" to mean "turn from sins" then this presentation is *unbiblical.* It is impossible for a sinner to fully believe in Jesus alone for salvation when he also believes his willpower to stop sinning also plays a part in obtaining salvation. You cannot trust in Jesus alone if you are also trusting in yourself.

On the other hand, if the writer of this presentation used the word "repent" to mean "turn from unbelief to belief," it is saying something true. To be saved, a person must turn from unbelief in Jesus to belief in Him.

Tricky stuff, isn't it? Now that you've made your way slowly and carefully through your assessment of these five "gospel" statements of beliefs, what do you think? I am sure you've seen the variety of perspectives that churches are teaching regarding the Gospel. Depending on what version of the Gospel a person hears and believes—the *Biblical* or *Unbiblical* version—it will determine whether they are truly saved or not. In any given church, there are three types of people present:

- **CATEGORY 1:** People who have accepted the Gospel and are saved. (Believers)
- **CATEGORY 2:** People who haven't yet chosen to accept the Gospel and are not saved. (Unbelievers)
- **CATEGORY 3:** People who have accepted a *false Gospel*—and are still not saved. (Still Unbelievers)

This *third* category of churchgoers is produced by false "gospel" presentations that demand people turn away from all their sins before they can be saved. This false requirement places the focus squarely on our works rather than on Jesus' finished work on the cross. Yes, it is good for a believer to turn away from their sins out of gratitude for the gift of salvation, but cleaning up our act is *not* a condition for salvation because we could never obtain it through obeying God's laws. Jesus plus nothing else will result in our salvation. Let's get this one straight because our eternal destiny depends on it.

Chapter 8

LIKE AN EVIL KITTEN-BEATER

*Blind Pharisee! First clean the inside of the cup
and dish, and then the outside also will be clean. Woe to
you, teachers of the law and Pharisees, you hypocrites! You are like
whitewashed tombs, which look beautiful on the outside but on the
inside are full of the bones of the dead and everything unclean. In
the same way, on the outside you appear to people as righteous
but on the inside you are full of hypocrisy and wickedness.*
Matthew 23:26–28, NIV

SOMETIMES YOU JUST CAN'T WIN

IT'S INCREDIBLY DIFFICULT to help a person trapped in the sin of self-righteousness. It's a bit like looking out a window in the Kansas prairie lands and seeing your blind neighbor picking flowers in a field—right underneath a forming tornado dropping from the clouds above. You run out the front door and scream out to your oblivious acquaintance: "Stop picking the flowers! You're going to get killed! Run this way!" Misunderstanding your concern, the sightless neighbor retorts: "Excuse me! What's your problem with my innocent activity? No one in their right mind would find fault with me picking flowers and enjoying a beautiful day. I don't need all your noise in my ear, so let me continue in peace." With this, you frantically continue, "No, no, you're misunderstanding me. I'm not upset with your flower picking. There's a real tornado about to drop down right on your head! Stop what you're doing and run over here to safety!" Sadly, the flower-picker carelessly yells back one last time, "Listen, I don't know why you want me to stop picking flowers. You're a disturbed soul. Go back inside and let me be."

HOW DO YOU CONFRONT GOOD BEHAVIOR?

It's one thing to walk up to a total pagan with a sin-destroyed life and tell him he needs a Savior. Here the problem is obvious, and the solution is unmistakably needed. However, it is a whole new beast to stand before a deeply "religious" person who has put massive amounts of time and energy into behavior purification and tell her that she should stop trusting in moral performance and put her full faith in the Savior for salvation. The pagan may grunt at you, but the self-righteous person often responds with a tirade that sounds a bit like this:

> "What is your problem? I love Jesus. I love church. I model my life after Jesus. I even try to think like Jesus. I am committed to what is good, and I shun what is evil. In fact, I am probably a better person than you are. What is your problem with my godly life? Back off!"

Here you see an offense has occurred. The true evangelist comes with a message to forsake trusting in good works for salvation, urging everyone to turn to the Savior, yet he is accused of fighting against godliness. This is not the case.

Nevertheless, the call to trust in the mercy of Jesus rather than in behavioral performance insults the pride of the self-righteous religious folk. Nothing bothers the self-saver more than hearing a true evangelist sing the words to that old song, "Nothing in my hand I bring, simply to the cross I cling."[3] In response, the self-righteous cry out with a vengeance, "Certainly a man must do something to be saved. If salvation were a gift, completely apart from the quality of our behavior, people would think they had a license to sin. Mister Evangelist, Jesus will not save a man unless he purifies himself of sin and does good!" What they are saying beneath the surface is they believe they are good enough for God. Here they make the true evangelist out to be the antagonist.

The evangelist must keep moving forward. Yes, confronting self-righteousness is worse than confronting a wolf in sheep's clothing. Imagine that you were taking a walk through your community park and saw a wolf disguised to look like a kitten. Out of concern for yourself and others, you would justifiably pick up the nearest stick and hit the "kitty," yelling and making a commotion to scare it off and warn others. How would you, a true hero, be perceived by the people who weren't in on the reality of the danger? You'd look like an evil kitten-beater! This is exactly how the true evangelist looks when he points at the religious-looking False "Gospel" of Morality and declares, "This is dangerous! You will not possess salvation if you try to be saved by all these good things you do!" Although the true evangelist faces this opposition, he must keep trucking on due to his love for people and obedience to the Savior's message.

---

[3] Toplady, Augustus. "Rock of Ages, Cleft for Me," https://www.hymnsite.com/lyrics/umh361.sht

TRUE DISCIPLESHIP BEGINS WHEN WE REJECT SELF-RIGHTEOUSNESS AND ACCEPT MERCY

A person's real relationship with Jesus begins precisely at that place where they drop their trust in Christ-like behavior to save them and trust in the real Savior *Himself.* Salvation comes through a Person, not through an act performed. Should you behave like Christ? Yes! But should you think your Christ-like behavior has a thing to do with making you right with God? NO! If you have been convinced you must *behave to be saved,* then you haven't yet understood a thing about the biblical concept of salvation.

You cannot be a genuine follower of Jesus if you haven't trusted Him as the one and only Savior, rejecting every single drop of self-righteousness within you. If you only determine to purify your thoughts and deeds, you will never be worthy of being called a disciple of Christ—you will forever be a proud, self-righteous Pharisee in Jesus' eyes. These people may have a clean outer life for the world to see, but their internal sin records will forever be filthy unless they trust in Jesus *exclusively* for salvation. This is the only way to free them from the legal guilt of their sins.

Readers, the self-righteous person I am describing used to be me. I was one of these people for much of my religious life. Then I finally ran to the Savior and said, "Save me, Jesus! I have nothing to add to You anymore!" I ask you to please do the same. You must filter the self-righteous mud out of the water before it becomes drinkable. You must strain every speck of self-righteousness out of your attempts to be saved to become acceptable to God.

Part 3

THE GOSPEL COMING INTO FOCUS

Chapter 9

GOD'S MIGHTY METAPHOR

I F YOU SEARCHED across the world's religions, you'd find a dizzying amount of metaphors to describe how a person can get himself or herself into right standing and peace with the Deity. Many people have said: "Getting to heaven is like a ladder a person must diligently climb," or "If you want to make it to the home of the gods above, you must consider a balance, making sure your good outweighs your bad, tipping the scale in your favor." Not all metaphors accurately describe the truth as God sees it, so it becomes our important task to figure out which perspective is really God's. So which metaphor best describes God's plan for getting into heaven? Thankfully, the Author of Salvation has written a book with clear answers accessible to anyone willing to look.

GOD'S FAVORITE METAPHOR

Sprinkled throughout the historical records of Scripture, God has consistently used one metaphor above all others to describe His plan for salvation: the metaphor of *sacrifice*. To be clear, the term "sacrifice" means *punishing an innocent substitute in the place of the guilty sinner.* Ouch! Sounds harsh. Nevertheless, this was the mighty metaphor God used to describe the Gospel from the earliest days of human existence. In fact, sacrifice was really God's *only* metaphor for describing His plan for our salvation. It's kind of like a drama with prophetic meaning. Let's look at several examples of God's special prophetic metaphor as it appears in the Bible:

- **ADAM AND EVE.** God Himself dealt with humanity's first sin while they were in the Garden of Eden. By personally sacrificing an animal, God used its skin to cover the effects of the sin of humans: the awareness and shame of their nakedness. This is the first record of death and bloodshed on planet earth, and this was completed by the hands of God. This was *sacrifice*—the innocent animal dying to cover the effects of sin. (Read Genesis 3:21)

- **CAIN AND ABEL.** With Cain and Able, God rejected Cain's offering of fruit; however, He fully accepted Abel's sacrifice of the life and blood of an innocent animal. (Read Genesis 4:2–4) God accepted Abel's sacrifice because it matched God's metaphor for the Gospel. Sacrifice was designed by God to symbolically appease God's anger against sin, and Cain failed to approach God through sacrifice. He should have learned from the example his parents, Adam and Eve, taught him.

- **ABRAHAM AND ISAAC.** God told Abraham to take his son Isaac up to a mountain and sacrifice him there. God stopped Abraham before he went through with it, but God wanted to use this prophetic act as symbolism for the ultimate salvation plan He was preparing to reveal in the future: the act of sacrificing Jesus, the Son of God. Interestingly enough, Jerusalem and the temple were built up on this same mountain in later centuries, and Jesus would eventually be crucified there. (Read Genesis 22:1–14)

- **THE TEMPLE AND THE LAMB.** God told the Israelites that when one member of their society sinned, the sinner was to select a spotless lamb and walk it to the temple altar. There he or she would lay hands on its head and confess that sin, and in an act of *substitution*, punish the innocent lamb for the sinner's sin-crime. This was *sacrifice*. (Read Leviticus 1:1–13)

- **THE PROPHET ISAIAH.** God compelled the prophet Isaiah to write that the Messiah-Savior would someday come and die like a lamb sacrifice, and that "the Lord has laid on Him the sin of us all" (Read Isaiah 53).

- **JOHN THE BAPTIST AND JESUS.** God sent a prophet named John from the priestly family, and his God-given job was to publicly point out the Messiah-Savior when He finally arrived. When Jesus finally showed up on the scene, God revealed this was the chosen rescuer who had long been foretold. John pointed at Jesus and declared: "There is the Lamb of God who has come to take away the sins of the world" (Read John 1:29).

We see the concept of *sacrifice* is inescapable throughout the Bible. There is good reason for this: God wanted to help us understand the Gospel, which was God's great rescue plan to remove the guilt of sinners, reconcile them to Himself, free them from eternity in hell, and earn them a place in heaven with Him forever.

The metaphor of sacrifice is God's chosen metaphor for salvation—the only metaphor God has approved and propagated. Again, if you want to summarize this concept of sacrifice, you might say sacrifice is *the punishment of the innocent in the place of the guilty.*

Since the first blood that spilled on earth in Eden with the first sacrifice of an animal, God already knew what He would do thousands of years later on a wooden cross in Jerusalem. The idea was the innocent Messiah-Savior would eventually die in place of guilty sinners, and He would bear their punishment for their guilt so they wouldn't have to. Magnificent! It is no wonder that we read the Scriptures beautifully declaring the good news: "For God presented Jesus as the sacrifice for sin. People are made right with God when they believe that Jesus sacrificed his life, shedding his blood" (Romans 3:25, NLT).

This perfect Savior willingly took the punishment for our sins upon His body as He hung on the cross. He was our Substitute, bearing all the punishment for our sins of commission (things we shouldn't have done) along with our often-undetected sins of omission (things we should have done but didn't do). Here is one of my favorite verses, and it describes this very thing. Pay close attention to what it says about the list of sins we earned through our bad choices. It says:

> God made [us] alive with Christ. He forgave us all our sins, having canceled the charge of our legal indebtedness, which stood against us and condemned us; he has taken it away, nailing it to the cross.
> Colossians 2:13–14, NIV

In the ancient days of Roman crucifixions, the criminals' crimes were written on parchment and nailed to the wood above their heads. The offenders would be sure to be hung in a public place. Everyone passing by could look up and read the reason for the executions. Jesus never sinned, yet as we just read, He essentially took our record of sin-debt that stood against us and allowed it to be nailed to His cross above His head—and then He died, being fully punished for our crimes against God.

What is the result of all this for the one who believes in this heaven-authorized Savior? The believer is left sinless—absolutely guilt-free in the sight of God! So Jesus was the ultimate Sacrifice, and He gave His life for us.

WALK YOUR LAMB TO THE ALTAR

How should this knowledge of God's mighty metaphor of sacrifice affect our lives? We should always make sure the Gospel message we accept and promote looks very much like the metaphor of sacrifice—the innocent taking the guilt and punishment for the guilty.

Our Gospel should not be illustrated by a ladder we must climb or by a scale for weighing our good works against our bad. If someone explains any so-called "gospel" presentation by the illustration of a *balance* for weighing good and bad works, reject that counterfeit immediately—it's no Gospel at all, and it's a danger to your soul. *Sacrifice* is God's mighty metaphor for His Gospel, and any supposed method of being right with God that doesn't look like sacrifice should be quickly tossed out the window of a moving car.

For those of us who believe this Gospel, we must think of Jesus as being the "Lamb" we bring to the altar of God as if we were offering Jesus as the sacrifice for our sins. It is sad Jesus had to die for our sin guilt, but there was truly no other way. We could never have done anything to dismiss God's wrath against our sinful actions and thoughts or do anything to clear our record.

Thankfully, Jesus has already died once and for all, taking the full punishment for our sins, so we don't have to. Today, with the knowledge of all Jesus did for us on the cross, let every one of us go to God without an ounce of trepidation, and confidently tell Him that we accept Jesus' death as the full sacrifice for all our sins. We can say, "God, thank You for sending Jesus to be punished for our guilt in our place. Upon these grounds, I know all my sin has already been punished, and I do not need to fear Your wrath anymore. Thank You for making a way for me to be reconciled to You." This is the Gospel perspective God recognizes and blesses, and it's the only way His wrath toward our sin will ever subside. If anyone accepts Jesus' sacrifice, that person will receive forgiveness of sins, reconciliation to God, and an eternal home in heaven. This is good news!

— Chapter 10 —

ISAIAH 53 AND THE GREAT "AWSHAM"

W HO BESIDES GOD can predict what the future has in store? *No one can.* Only God knows the future. Seven hundred years before Jesus was ever born, God had already begun marvelously predicting in-depth details about the coming of the Messiah-Savior He would eventually send. The blueprints for His entire plan were already in place long before it came into existence. This provides amazing proof for those wondering if Jesus is really a Savior sent from God to save us from our sins.

So where exactly can we go to find these predictions? There is no better place to look than the 53rd chapter of Isaiah. Isaiah was a Jewish prophet who relayed God's divine messages to the world, and this incredible chapter is directly quoted in the New Testament seven times, including Matthew 8:14–17, Luke 22:35–38, John 12:37–38, Acts 8:26–38, Romans 10:16, and 1 Peter 2:19–25. Now let's take a look at Isaiah's message. As you read through this fascinating chapter, think about each detail predicted about the coming Savior. What is He like? What happens to Him? What is the stated purpose for all that happens to Him? As you read, don't forget this chapter was written seven centuries before Jesus came into the world.

ISAIAH 53

Who has believed our message and to whom has the arm of the LORD been revealed? He grew up before him like a tender shoot, and like a root out of dry ground. He had no beauty or majesty to attract us to him, nothing in his appearance that we should desire him. <u>He was despised and rejected by mankind</u>, a man of suffering, and familiar with pain. Like one from whom people hide their faces he was despised, and we held him low in esteem. Surely he took up our pain and bore our suffering, yet we considered him punished by God, stricken by him, and afflicted. But <u>he was pierced for our transgressions</u>, he was <u>crushed for our iniquities</u>; the punishment that brought us peace was on him, and by his wounds we are healed. We all, like sheep, have gone astray, each of us has turned to our own way; and <u>the LORD has laid on him the iniquity of us all</u>. He was oppressed and afflicted, yet he did not open his mouth; <u>he was led like a lamb to the slaughter</u>, and as a sheep before its shearers is silent, so he did not open his mouth. By oppression and judgment he was taken away. Yet who of his generation protested? For he was cut off from the land of the living; for the transgression of my people he was punished. He was <u>assigned a grave with the wicked</u>, and <u>with the rich in his death</u>, though he had done no violence, nor was any deceit in his mouth. Yet <u>it was the LORD's will to crush him and cause him to suffer</u>, and though <u>the LORD makes his life an offering for sin</u>, he will see his offspring and prolong his days, and the will of the LORD will prosper in his hand. <u>After he has suffered, he will see the light of life</u> and be satisfied; by his knowledge my righteous servant will justify many, and <u>he will bear their iniquities</u>. Therefore I will give him a portion among the great, and he will divide the spoils with the strong, because he poured out his life unto death, and was numbered with the transgressors. For he bore the sin of many, and made intercession for the transgressors.

Isaiah 53:1–12, NIV

This is in the Bible, and we should think carefully about every word. If the all-knowing God speaks a message, every word and thought matters. This prophetic passage speaks about the Messiah God would eventually send; about the way He would be despised and rejected when He came; how He would be wounded, bruised, and beaten; that He would die with the wicked, but be buried with the rich; that He would come back to life again. How did the prophet Isaiah know what would happen with such clarity? The answer is God predicted it. God had everything planned long before it happened.

THE DAY OF ATONEMENT IN A BROOKLYN SYNAGOGUE

I went with my Jewish friend to the local synagogue in Park Slope, Brooklyn, a couple of years back. This day happened to be the most solemn annual holiday on the Jewish calendar: The Day of Atonement. (The word *atonement* means a covering over of sins so that God no longer sees them) On this somber day, religious Jews diligently fast from all food and water to devote their entire day to the confession of sins before God. You would have to see it to believe it. Literally, every category of sin imaginable is brought up and confessed. If you ever have the chance, I highly recommend attending one of these fascinating gatherings.

During a break in the religious activities of this day of confession, my Jewish friend and I sat at a table, and I pulled out my Bible. I opened it to Isaiah chapter 53 and slid the book over to him. "Read this," I said. Knowing little about the Bible, and not believing Jesus could ever be the Jewish Messiah-Savior, my friend read it over and then passed it back to me. "Who is this talking about?" I asked him. "Jesus, obviously" he replied, thinking he had been reading from the "Christian" part of the Bible. "Scott," I said, "this passage you just read is in the book of Isaiah—a Jewish prophet from the Hebrew Scriptures. It's in the Old Testament and was written seven hundred years before Jesus was born. Think about what you said." He turned white as a ghost with this realization. My good friend had come so close to the truth, but his family upbringing wouldn't allow him to entertain these thoughts about Jesus much further. I love my friend and will continue to be there for him, no matter what he ultimately determines about his relationship to Jesus.

THE GREAT "AWSHAM"

One of the most amazing aspects of Isaiah 53 lies hidden deep within the original Hebrew language far out of sight for most English speakers. In the middle of verse 10, we read God uses the life of the subject of this passage as a "guilt offering." After translating this term back into the original Hebrew language, we find the word "awsham." This startling and powerful word is so rich in meaning it must be defined. Religiously observant Jews living in the days of the ancient Jewish temple in Jerusalem were well acquainted with the practice of bringing a lamb to the temple of God, confessing their sin over the lamb, and then watching as a priest slashed the lamb with a sharp blade across the neck. It was essentially instant death for the lamb, and as the blood poured out over the temple altar, the sinless lamb would be seen as bearing the guilt and full punishment for the sinner's offenses against God. Although this custom may sound strange to modern ears, this type of sacrifice was precisely what God required the ancient Jewish people to do when they sinned.

The Hebrew word awsham that translators interpreted as "guilt offering" is the exact name the Israelites used for these animal sacrifices that were brought to the temple to be executed in place of humans who had sinned against God's law.[4] With this cultural background now brought to light, why do you think God prompted the prophet Isaiah to call the suffering Messiah an "awsham"?

The lamb sacrifices served as a prophetic "dress rehearsal" for the true Savior who would eventually come and bear the sins of sinners. In the tenth verse of this 53rd chapter of Isaiah, we see a declaration that God deliberately chose to use the Messiah as a *sin sacrifice* for the people—like the lambs in the temple were used. This is what the entire death on the cross event was all about. It was about reconciling you and me to the God who loves us and wants to be in perfect relationship with us. We are offered forgiveness and a full pardon through the cross because another person has already paid our punishment in full.

WHAT SHOULD WE DO ABOUT IT?

Nobody can tell the future—except God. Seven hundred years before Jesus' birth, God knew He would send this great Savior to take the punishment for our sins upon Himself, giving His innocent

---

[4] "H817 – 'asham – Strong's Hebrew Lexicon (KJV)." Blue Letter Bible. https://www.blueletterbible.org//lang/lexicon/lexicon.cfm?Strongs=H817&t=KJV

life up so that sinners like you and me could be saved. Reading Isaiah 53 provides astounding proof for the world that God had His master plan of salvation cooking in the oven all along, and Jesus was His living, walking, breathing, dying, and resurrecting Master Plan. Now our sins can be completely removed from our records if we will believe and accept Jesus' sacrificial death on the cross as the payment for our sins. Confessing our sins will never fix the problem; instead, we need true *atonement*—a valid covering over of our sins so God will no longer see them and hold them against us. Atonement is God's will for all sinners, and the Bible makes this clear when it proclaims that "the LORD has laid on Him the iniquity of us all" (Isaiah 53:6, NIV).

If we will only make Jesus our sacrificial Lamb, God will honor this sacrifice in our place and consider our sin debt as paid in full whether you were brought up Jewish or "Christian" or any other tradition. If you haven't yet, accept Jesus as your Savior now. Your eternal destiny rests on how you deal with the Jesus question. If you ever hope to have your sins atoned for (covered over), to be reconciled to God, and to gain a place in heaven forever, this mighty Savior must be the bull's eye of your faith and the linchpin of your salvation—the One it's all about and the One who holds it all together.

— *Chapter 11* —

FORGIVENESS THROUGH A CROSSLESS GOSPEL?

Jesus told him, "I am the way, the truth, and the life.
No one can come to the Father except through me.
John 14:6, NLT

I MAGINE A COURTROOM SCENE where a criminal stands in terror before a judge, awaiting severe sentencing for the crimes he has committed. The offender fervently pleads, "Good judge, you seem like a deeply *loving* and *merciful* person. If you really are these things, then I ask you to pardon me from the guilt and punishment I deserve for my crimes. I ask you to drop the charges and let me go free." The friends and family of the criminal crowd the courtroom and everyone anxiously await the judge's response. The judge replies:

> "Yes, it's true: I am a loving and merciful person. But you must understand I am also a judge—a *good* judge—and I must faithfully uphold justice in everything I do. You are guilty of defiantly breaking the law. For me to disregard *justice* in the name of *love* and *mercy* would be *unjust*."

JUSTICE MUST BE UPHELD

In this allegory, the criminal represents a sinner (like you or me) who attempts to seek forgiveness from the God of the Universe by appealing to His love and mercy. Some people are convinced that God's love and mercy will compel Him to drop the charges of sin that stand against them, thinking, "God's love and mercy will override His interest in judging sin." However, this is a dangerous gamble and one that has no scriptural basis. The love and mercy of God are amazing. The Bible makes it clear God has a deep love for us, and that mercy is one of His prominent qualities. In the same way, the judge responded in our illustration; God refuses to allow love and mercy to override His justice. The love and desire for mercy may throb in God's heart, but His perfect justice compels the Judge's gavel to swing down with a deafening crash, condemning sin wherever it is found.

If God let sin off the hook, He would err greatly, and through this, He would destroy His holiness—something He will never do. We naturally understand this concept even with our earthly judges. We all know that any earthly judge who allows crimes to go unpunished is not worthy to sit in a judge's seat of authority. If this is true of our judges here on earth, why should we expect it to be any different with God above?

The Bible declares every human being on the planet has sinned and fallen below heaven's perfect standard. We read:

> There is no one righteous, not even one; there is no one who understands; there is there is no one who seeks God. All

have turned away, they have together become worthless; there is no one who does good, not even one.
Romans 3:10–12, NIV

If we are honest with our self-assessment and take the previous Scripture passage seriously, we must all admit we each stand as the criminal in the previous story: desiring pardon, yet standing utterly guilty before the Judge. Without help, we are truly without hope—destined to one day receive the condemnation and sentencing we deserve.

GOD'S BRILLIANT ARRANGEMENT

Despite our grave sin problem, there is spectacular news for us! In the most amazing rescue mission of all time, God engineered an ingenious plan that allows Him to perfectly uphold His wonderful traits of *love* and *mercy* while simultaneously upholding His perfect *justice*. Pay attention carefully: While God was compelled by His justice to execute the full punishment against our sin-crimes, His amazing love and mercy compelled Him to seek a way to free us from this punishment we deserved. Yes, our Judge implemented a plan to justly uphold the penalty for our crimes to the letter of the law while legally sparing us from the condemnation we were due. He did this by arranging for sinless Jesus to step onto the scene to bear the full wrath and punishment of the law. Jesus essentially jumped between us and the Law, and God executed the punishment we deserved upon Jesus so that He wouldn't have to punish us. Jesus was the Great Substitute. This is how God demonstrates His perfect justice while simultaneously pouring out His love and mercy on us.

APPROACH GOD BY WAY OF THE CROSS

Many people approach God for forgiveness through their custom-made paths. However, it is critically important to understand any approach besides God's authorized approach will be rejected due to His justice. To escape the judgment due us and achieve forgiveness and right standing with God, we must make our way to God through the only path He has ever made available to us: Jesus. The Holy Scriptures have taken heaven's spotlight and pointed it directly upon God's chosen doorway to heaven, declaring of Jesus:

> There is no other name under heaven given among men by which we must be saved.
> Acts 4:12, NKJV

There you have it: There is no other way for us to get to God unless we go through Jesus. No other path will do. If a person could have received forgiveness by requesting it of God, why on earth would God have sent Jesus to go to the cross for us? If we all could have gone directly to God to ask Him for a pardon from sin based only on His love and mercy, why would Jesus have needed to die in our place? It was God's *love* and *mercy* that caused Him to make salvation available through Jesus. The Savior said: "Greater love has no one than this: to lay down one's life for one's friends" (John 15:13, NIV). This love propelled Jesus to the cross to rescue us.

When we approach God to ask for forgiveness of sins, we must remember to ask in Jesus' name, firmly based on the fact that Jesus experienced our punishment for us as a substitute. Our appeal for forgiveness should look something like this:

"Heavenly Father, I now ask You to grant me forgiveness for my sins—a full pardon. I ask You to hear and honor this request because of what Jesus, Your chosen Savior, did for me. I know Jesus took upon Himself the full punishment for all my sins when He hung and died on the cross. Because He was already punished in my place for my sins, I know there is no longer any need for me to be condemned or punished. I now place my full faith in Jesus as my personal Savior, taking full advantage of this gift of salvation You offer me through Him. Forgive me of all my sins because of what Jesus did for me. Amen."

God definitely loves us and wants us to ask for a pardon, but we must do this on the grounds He has prepared for us. This is how we should come to God to seek pardon, and it is the only way our request will be heard and honored. Ask for forgiveness of sins in Jesus' name.

Chapter 12

BOILING IT DOWN TO THE RAW ESSENCE OF THE GOSPEL

WHAT WOULD YOU SAY if an unbelieving family member you loved was on his or her deathbed and asked you the question, "How can I know for certain I will go to heaven when I die?" How would you answer if *you* were the one asking the question with only moments left to live? Without a doubt, it is incredibly important for us to be able to answer this question, both for ourselves and for others around us. If you were to boil down all the religious clichés and conversational fat until nothing was left but the very essence of the Gospel, what exactly would you have left? Thankfully, God gave us a clear answer.

The biblical story of Cornelius is a spectacular case study for analyzing the raw essence of the salvation message. Why is this story so perfect for our purpose? Because the Bible says a man named Peter walked into the house of an "unsaved" man named Cornelius, then Peter gave a short sermon, and then Cornelius was "saved" by the end of that sermon. Because this was so, it makes sense that the message Peter spoke had 100 percent of the necessary truth components to a get a person saved. We won't overlook this God-given case study.

PETER'S SAVING SERMON

Let's have a close look at the words from Peter's sermon. As we move along, see if you can identify some main components of Peter's important message. Here we go:

> God anointed Jesus of Nazareth with the Holy Spirit and with power, who went about doing good and healing all who were oppressed by the devil, for God was with Him. And we are witnesses of all things which He did both in the land of the Jews and in Jerusalem, whom <u>they killed by hanging on a tree.</u> <u>Him God raised up on the third day</u>, and showed Him openly, not to all the people, but to witnesses chosen before by God, even to us who ate and drank with Him after He arose from the dead. And He commanded us to preach to the people, and to testify that it is He who was ordained by God to be Judge of the living and the dead. To Him all the prophets witness that, <u>through His name, whoever believes in Him will receive remission of sins.</u>
> Acts 10:38–43, NKJV

That's it. That's the exact short sermon (minus the introduction) Cornelius heard and believed. The Scriptures declare the moment Cornelius believed this message he was "saved." How do we know this? Well, the next verse following Peter's sermon declares: "While Peter was still speaking these words, the Holy Spirit fell upon all those who heard the word" (Acts 10:44, NKJV). People only get the Holy Spirit of God when they are forgiven and saved, so that sermon must have had all the ingredients necessary to save a person!

THE MESSAGE THAT SAVES

Now that we see the incredible outcome of the message Peter preached to Cornelius, let's analyze the main components of this message. Here is a quick summary of the Gospel Peter gave to Cornelius:

1. Jesus died on the cross.
2. God raised Jesus back to life three days later.
3. Anyone who believes in Jesus' sin-atoning death will receive a full pardon from their sins.

That's it! No religious clichés or conversational fat—just the beautiful, raw essence of the *Gospel*! Peter told Cornelius how Jesus had died on the cross and resurrected three days later, and that we get a full pardon for our sins when we believe Jesus did this for us. This is a perfect reminder that salvation has and always will be obtained through faith in Jesus.

THE SIMPLE, WONDERFUL GOSPEL

Is it really as easy as that? Absolutely! All we have to do is believe—nothing more, nothing less. But as we receive this gift of salvation through faith, let us never forget what a massive price Jesus had to pay for us to be forgiven from our sins, reconciled to God, and given an eternal place in heaven. How could we ever ask for more?

Part 4

THE PLACE OF OBEDIENCE IN A WORLD OF GRACE

Chapter 13

THE ROOTS OF FAITH AND
THE FRUITS OF GODLY BEHAVIOR

For it is by grace you have been saved, through faith—
and this is not from yourselves, it is the gift of God—
not by works, so that no one can boast.
Ephesians 2:8–9, NIV

J UST AS IT is irrational to believe fruit could ever appear on a
tree before the roots form, so it is foolish to believe a person
could ever produce the authentic fruit of godly behavior
before the existence of the roots of faith. The Bible explains
the order in which this process takes place: First the inner change,
then the outer change. We read:

> I will give you a new heart and put a new spirit in you; I will
> remove from you your heart of stone and give you a heart of
> flesh. And I will put my Spirit in you and move you to
> follow my decrees and be careful to keep my laws.
> Ezekiel 36:26–27, NIV

A miracle occurs at the point of faith due to something miraculous
God does in us. Some call this the "born again" experience, this

term being inspired by the third chapter of the book of John. When we trust in Jesus and His sacrificial work on the cross as that thing that earns us our forgiveness and right standing before God, God accepts us and puts His Holy Spirit in us. With the Holy Spirit living within us and helping us, it then becomes much more natural to follow God's ways than it ever was before. After a person believes, the first signs of fruit are sometimes tiny and seemingly insignificant. New believers will often mature and grow in their faith through the nourishment of the sunlight of God's presence, the watering of God's Word, and the help of the Holy Spirit, and some believers may eventually produce a full harvest of fruit. The Bible declares: "But the Holy Spirit produces this kind of fruit in our lives: love, joy, peace, patience, kindness, goodness, faithfulness, gentleness, and self-control" (Galatians 5:22–23, NLT).

THE ONGOING STRUGGLE

Remember, despite being born again and having the help of the Holy Spirit from within, a believer will continue to wrestle with the sinful cravings and lusts of his mortal body as long as he is alive. Once a person is saved and becomes a child of God, the Holy Spirit comes to live inside of that person, and He will encourage a whole new way of living. However, a person's old sinful nature within the body continues to live on until the end of life.

Before salvation, it isn't much of a fight when the sinful cravings of our mortal bodies act up. However, after a person is born again and receives the gift of the Holy Spirit, a believer is no longer *compelled* to sin like he was before. It's as if there is a man in chains of slavery, unable to walk far from his place of bondage, and suddenly someone comes and cuts the chains, disconnects the ties to the old dark place, and the slave walks free. He no longer needs to stay near the place of his past slavery. It is similar in the life of an unbeliever set free from the guilt of sin and receives the Holy Spirit of God. That person has a new heart and experiences new desires. Now a real resistance can take place against the sinful nature, and the Holy Spirit of God gives the power to win that battle. It could be said it is like going from being an animal that grazes eating the grass and weeds in a field to becoming a human with a human appetite. The craving for the old things seems to lose its attraction as the Holy Spirit helps us from within to change our thinking and desires.

LIKE A PIG IN THE PEN

It is important to remember a person's identity is changed when he places full faith in Jesus' finished work on the cross. It is a bit like this: before a person places his trust in Jesus, he is actually a pig rolling around in the Pigpen of Sin. As a pig, it feels natural to eat slop, and nothing feels more normal than to be covered in mud from head to toe with the rest of the pigs. When a person gets saved, it is like that pig miraculously becomes a human. That person wakes up to the fact he is a human down on his hands and knees, wallowing in the filth. This new believer may continue to live in the same condition as he did before, but as long as he holds on to his faith in Jesus, he will never again feel truly at home rolling around with the rest of the pigs in the pigpen. Rather, after being saved, the more natural tendency is to stand up, wipe the mud off his face, and climb out of the pen altogether.

You better believe the Holy Spirit will lovingly teach, correct, and even chastise those who are children of God. Hebrews 12:5–11 has a lot to say on this topic. With this said, we must be patient with each other—especially with new believers. Yes, the roots of faith come in an instant, upon belief; yet sometimes it takes a new believer quite some time to produce the fruit—especially if they lack a strong support system. Each of us should always trust in Jesus' finished work on the cross alone for our salvation and lovingly encourage each other to let the Holy Spirit produce a rich harvest of the fruits of godly behavior in our lives. This rich harvest is God's will for all His children who are saved by grace.

"BELIEVERS" WHO DON'T SHOW ANY FRUIT

Some may ask: "What about those people who claim to be 'believers' yet produce no fruit at all?" Some people mingle around in the community of believers who live every bit like an unbeliever. These certain individuals do not seem to take any heed to the way God expects His children to live, and continue to show evidence they feel at home in the Pigpen of Sin.

Although these people claim the title "believer" by name, if we see no fruit in them, then we could reasonably suspect they don't have the roots of true faith. These people may never have actually been saved by putting their faith in Jesus' sacrificial death. They may attend religious functions, go through religious motions, and enjoy the companionship of true believers, yet they might not have ever trusted Jesus for their salvation. Read this next statement carefully: *It isn't that they aren't true believers because they behave poorly; instead, they aren't true believers because they don't have faith.* Faith in Jesus' finished work on the cross saves a person and makes someone a true *believer.* The Bible helps us to understand this in the following passage:

Anyone who continues to live in him will not sin. But anyone who keeps on sinning does not know him or understand who he is. Dear children, don't let anyone deceive you about this: When people do what is right, it shows that they are righteous, even as Christ is righteous. But when people keep on sinning, it shows that they belong to the devil, who has been sinning since the beginning. But the Son of God came to destroy the works of the devil. Those who have been born into God's family do not make a practice of sinning, because God's life is in them. So they can't keep on sinning, because they are children of God.
1 John 3:6–9, NLT

Believers who have trusted in Jesus as Savior are righteous in God's sight; their sins have been forgiven, and the Holy Spirit lives in them. They have been "born again" spiritually, made new from the inside, and the Holy Spirit gives them constant guidance and strength to think differently toward sin. The Bible tells us there will be plenty of people who socialize in the faith community who claim to be believers yet aren't really people of faith. It should not surprise believers that these people still feel at home in the Pigpen of Sin. As strange as it is, the passage we read from 1 John explains that "when people keep on sinning, it shows that they belong to the devil..." The Greek verb used here translated as "keep on sinning"[5] suggests a continuous present tense engagement with sin, and suggests this unbeliever's inner desire toward sin is expressed in his habitual practice of it.

John is pointing out the contrast between the people who have trusted in Jesus and received the Holy Spirit and the people who

[5] "G264 - hamartanō – Strong's Greek Lexicon (KJV)." Blue Letter Bible.
https://www.blueletterbible.org//lang/lexicon/lexicon.cfm?Strongs=G264&t=KJV

have not: Those who have been saved through faith cannot keep on feeling at home in sin because they are "born again" from the inside and have the Holy Spirit living within. Those who have not been saved by faith are not "born again" and do not have the Holy Spirit living within; these people show this inner reality by their continued enjoyment of the Pigpen of sin. Note: We must be careful in our judgments regarding a person's faith because some struggling believers look a lot like the false believers I am talking about. Although it may be hard to tell the difference from the outside with these two people groups, there is an internal difference, and that difference is *faith*.

LOSING SALVATION

There are also some people out there who grapple with the question: "Does a true believer lose salvation if the fruits of godly behavior shrivel up in her life?" The answer is: Absolutely not. The believer does not earn or lose salvation through behavior—good or bad. Instead, it is through faith in Jesus' finished work on the cross that we are saved. If we see a person who once had saving faith in Jesus acting in ways that seem to contradict her faith, maybe this person has allowed deception into her life and has fallen away from her trust in the Savior, or she may just be making some foolish and harmful decisions. A believer doesn't lose salvation by sinful behavior. Sinful behavior doesn't make a believer unsaved any more than good behavior makes sinners saved.

However, a believer *will* lose her salvation if she loses her faith. Speaking to former believers, Paul says: "For if you are trying to make yourselves right with God by keeping the law, you have been cut off from Christ! You have fallen away from God's grace"

(Galatians 5:4, NLT). Paul is referring to people who had once trusted in Jesus but had ceased to continue trusting Him alone to save them. If a believer's faith roots die for any reason, making that person an *unbeliever*, it is no wonder the fruits of godly behavior quickly rot and wither away. Yet we never need to fear this as long as we continue to firmly trust in Jesus to save us. He is absolutely able to save us from the guilt of our sins as we trust in Him—even with all our weaknesses and failures.

SUMMARY

Now let's summarize what we have learned. The roots of faith come first, and it is by faith in Jesus' sacrificial work on the cross that a person has his or her sins completely removed. Jesus took the full punishment for every one of our sins upon Himself so that we would not need to be punished.

When a person believes in Jesus and receives forgiveness from God, the Holy Spirit then comes to live inside the new believer. Once the roots of faith appear at the moment of salvation, the new believer grows in maturity with the help of the Holy Spirit, and eventually, the fruits of godly behavior should appear. The Holy Spirit teaches and encourages the believer, gently leading him to align his behavior with God's Word. Salvation happens by faith apart from works— apart from good behavior and in spite of bad behavior. It's all about what Jesus did for us, and all we have to do is believe and accept what He did on our behalf.

Chapter 14

SIN'S COLLATERAL DAMAGE

N OBODY GAINS SALVATION through his behavior, and no believer loses salvation through his behavior. Salvation is *gained* and *maintained* exclusively through faith in Jesus' sacrificial death on the cross. So how should we deal with the reality of believers who sin in various degrees? Well, we should deal with it realistically.

THE REAL-WORLD DAMAGE OF SIN

Realistically speaking, sins committed after the point of salvation do nothing to the believer's official sin record. A believer's right standing with God and perfect legal righteousness stays intact, and sin guilt falls off a believer like water off a duck's back. However, sin inflicts great damage in the earthly life of believers who take part in it—and it negatively impacts others as well. It is impossible for a person to sin without having negative practical consequences appear somewhere. Let's take a look at several examples of sin along with their consequences:

- **LYING.** When you lie, it causes relational breakdown as others feel distrust toward you. Knowing you lied causes you to distrust others more, wondering if others are lying too.

- **THEFT.** Stealing has put locks on all modern doors. When you steal in big or small ways—robbing banks, fudging numbers for taxes, or failing to tithe—it robs God's ability to bless your finances. (See Malachi 3:7–12)

- **JEALOUSY.** Jealousy causes stressful competition and bitterness and strips your peace away.

- **PORNOGRAPHY.** Pornography harms intimacy and trust between a husband and wife, and it trains a person to be dissatisfied in normal, realistic relationships.

- **DISRESPECT.** Not caring for your needy parents in their old age teaches your kids how to treat you when you get old—and what goes around often comes around.

- **PRIDE.** The sin of pride will keep you from growing in wisdom, it will hurt relationships, and it will encourage soul-damaging obsession over self.

- **GREED.** The sin of greed causes humans to improperly pursue their gain with such obsession that gain comes at the expense of the well-being of others. Often greed results in the idolatry of self.

- **RACISM.** This is essentially a double-headed sin of ugly pride (thinking better of oneself than others) and mistreating people made in the image of God. Racism robs society of the peace and unity God desires for us.

- **SELF-CENTEREDNESS.** Turning a blind eye to the poor will cause you to eventually feel shallow and unfulfilled in your self-centeredness.

- **ADULTERY.** The sin of adultery often causes massive, far-reaching destruction in the lives of the husband, wife, and children of multiple family units.

- **FORNICATION.** Sexual sin causes mental havoc, relational bonds where they are not wanted, countless cases of disease, and millions of children born into homes that don't have both parents present.
- **UNFORGIVENESS.** The sin of unforgiveness often brings on anxiety, sleeping disorders, and emotional and physical disorders of many kinds.
- **HIDDEN SIN.** Hidden sin causes guilt, angst, and muddled fellowship with God.

As we can see from this short list, sin inflicts severe damage on our lives, destroying the peace, joy, and health God desires for His children. Figuratively speaking, when you sin you are essentially asking for the hurricane, tornado, and hailstorm to plow through your life. Sin causes you to step outside God's safety and protection, and it opens the door for the devil to harm you. I promise the effects of sin will not be fun.

THE RISK OF SHIPWRECKED FAITH

Now here is a sobering warning regarding sin that goes far beyond the consequences listed earlier, so readers beware. It is possible that extended periods of rebellion and continued disobedience to God could lead to profound spiritual weakness, and this weak condition could make the believer incredibly vulnerable to the deception of the devil, false doctrine, spiritual confusion, and possibly the eventual shipwrecking of their faith in Jesus.

I remember a friend who had at one time trusted Jesus fully for his salvation (as far as his words and actions exhibited). Sadly, through an extensive period of lack of self-discipline, avoidance of fellowship with other believers, and persistence in disobeying his conscience and the Holy Spirit's leading, my friend has now disregarded all belief in God and has completely renounced his faith in Jesus as Savior. I watched as his ongoing choices to indulge in sin brought on greater and greater guilt, spiritual weakness, and confusion. In the frail and sickly state of his soul, he became easy prey for the devil's lies and schemes. The fog of deception filled his mind, and eventually he no longer knew what he believed. He was a brilliant person, but it does not take brilliance to see God's truths; instead, it takes the teaching of God's Spirit. Today my friend is forcefully opposed to any thought of God and the Savior He sent. During one of my latest phone conversations with him he included a tirade of taunting and mocking statements thrown at Jesus. How could such a drastic shift in thinking occur? Sin took its heavy toll on my friend.

Losing faith is, of course, the one sin that leaves a person with no solution for sin. This is the sad story of a believer who had his faith shipwrecked by sin. Speaking exclusively of the sin of unbelief, the writer of Hebrews says:

> Therefore, brothers, since we have confidence to enter the holy places by the blood of Jesus, by the new and living way that he opened for us through the curtain, that is, through his flesh, and since we have a great priest over the house of God, let us draw near with a true heart in full assurance of faith, with our hearts sprinkled clean from an evil conscience and our bodies washed with pure water. <u>Let us hold fast the confession of our hope without wavering</u>, for he who promised is faithful. And let us consider how to stir up one another to love and good works, not neglecting to meet together, as is the habit of some, but encouraging one another, and all the more as you see the Day drawing near.

For if we go on sinning [the sin of unbelief] deliberately after receiving the knowledge of the truth, there no longer remains a sacrifice for sins, but a fearful expectation of judgment, and a fury of fire that will consume the adversaries. Anyone who has set aside the law of Moses dies without mercy on the evidence of two or three witnesses. How much worse punishment, do you think, will be deserved by the one who has trampled underfoot the Son of God, and has profaned the blood of the covenant by which he was sanctified, and has outraged the Spirit of grace? Hebrews 10:19–29, ESV (underline and brackets added for clarification of context)

Note: A careful reading of the book of Hebrews, along with the context of Hebrews chapter 10, reveals the central thesis of the entire book of Hebrews is to warn against the sin of *unbelief*. This context should be carefully considered. Here, in this passage, we see the possible consequence of sin at its worst!

BE ENCOURAGED

With all this said, be encouraged! You are saved through your faith in Jesus' sin-cleansing death on the cross. Continue to trust Him with all your heart, and you will never be condemned. Don't mess with the trap of sin with all the undesirable consequences that often come along with it. Sin is not good for you or others. Let the Holy Spirit lead you into ever-increasing obedience, wisdom, and spiritual maturity, learning every lesson He wants to teach you. When you sin, bounce right back up, knowing you have a Savior who can save you from all your sins.

Chapter 15

THE DISCIPLINE OF A LOVING FATHER

Those who spare the rod of discipline hate their children.
Those who love their children care enough to discipline them.
Proverbs 13:24, NLT

S ALVATION MAY VERY well be by faith, but does this mean we have a "license to sin"? This is an excellent question I believe naturally comes up when talking about salvation by faith. One of God's great interests is to see His children grow into spiritual adults who tame their desires with self-control and live good lives of honor and holiness. If left on our tendencies with no input from God's loving correction, we would probably spin out of control in our sin, live recklessly, and bring great disorder to others and ourselves. Thankfully, one clear biblical promise is every child of God will be disciplined by their heavenly Father when they need it. The Bible has some fascinating things to say about the kind heart of the Father and the purpose for His loving discipline:

> And have you forgotten the encouraging words God spoke to you as his children? He said, "My child, don't make light of the LORD'S discipline, and don't give up when he

corrects you. For the LORD disciplines those he loves, and he punishes each one he accepts as his child." As you endure this divine discipline, remember that God is treating you as his own children. Who ever heard of a child who is never disciplined by its father? If God doesn't discipline you as he does all his children, it means that you are illegitimate and are not really his children at all...

No discipline is enjoyable while it is happening—it's painful! But afterward there will be a peaceful harvest of right living for those who are trained in this way.
Hebrews 12:5–8, 11, NLT

When you stop and think about it, this passage tells us a whole lot about how God works. According to the Bible, God's discipline is proof He loves us, wants to help us develop into amazing people, and has our best interest in mind.

THE STORY OF LOVING DISCIPLINE

Some ask: Can saved people ever sin? Well, yes, we can—and we often do. We are saved by faith in the Savior's finished work on the cross, and this has nothing to do with our behavior and has everything to do with Jesus. But we must remember that God disciplines those He loves. Because we are much-loved children of God, we will hear from Him when we sin—especially if we are openly rebelling against Him with destructive choices. He will often start the process of discipline by gently pointing out where we have strayed, and by this, we should feel godly sorrow from the nudging from the Holy Spirit of God who lives inside us. However, if that does not work, the discipline will increase in intensity until God's desired result is accomplished. The goal of God's discipline is a full harvest of right living in us, which brings incredible benefits to everyone involved.

ARE WE FREE TO SIN?

Are believers who are saved by faith completely free to sin? Well, in a sense, they *are* because believers do not lose their salvation by sinning (unless it happens to be the sin of unbelief in the Savior). Those who believe in Jesus are saved by faith from start to finish. Yet in another sense, there is definitely a price to pay with Dad when a child of God misbehaves. This discipline reveals God's love for us! In fact, the most hateful thing God could do to His children would be to refuse to confront them when they strayed from the right path. This would show a complete lack of interest in their well-being. Like those spoiled, undisciplined children we periodically see throwing temper tantrums in the grocery store, we would never learn our lesson. God doesn't want this for us, and because of this love, He is willing to confront us. This is the story of the loving discipline of God.

— Chapter 16 —

WHAT'S MY MOTIVATION?

I N OUR FAITH communities, we often use the term "movement of God" when referring to trends of positive behavioral change taking place in our midst. But is every "movement of God" really something God is behind? I really wonder.

Imagine an alleged "movement of God" in which a moral reformation occurs across the entire congregation. With tears streaming down their faces, the crowd responds to the teaching from the pulpit on the importance of fleeing from sin. People are passionately casting away their drugs, needles, secret mistresses, tax evasions, and porn addictions—all the things that should definitely be rejected. A large percentage of the church is radically impacted, and the church leadership vigorously applauds "the work God is doing." By looking around the congregation and seeing positive lifestyle changes taking place en masse, many would never consider it anything else but a divine work in the hearts of His people.

While it may be true God is behind this, it might also be something other than God fueling this lifestyle change. We would need to dig a bit deeper to find out. Let's do it.

YEAH—BUT WHAT'S THE MOTIVATION?

While outward moral purification is good, perceptive believers must be careful to identify the true driving force behind the explosive positive behavioral change in a particular congregation. When we see great moral transformation taking place and many people becoming "better" imitators of Jesus, we must ask: Is the correct thing fueling this change? We should absolutely rejoice when we remove destructive sin from our lives—but we should remove it the correct way. For a cancerous growth, there is a right and a wrong way to remove it. Perhaps a scalpel in the hands of a careful surgeon could extract the problem in the right way, removing what needs to be removed while preserving the rest of the body. Destroying a cancerous growth with a military-grade flamethrower may eliminate it but destroy the body in the process. Similarly, there is a right and a wrong way to remove sin from our lives.

THREE THINGS THAT FUEL BEHAVIORAL REFORMATION

Not everything people describe as a "movement of God" is genuinely a movement of God. Three perspectives tend to fuel behavioral transformation in people within the religious community. Two of these fuel behavioral change for the wrong reasons; only one perspective fuels the right change. Below I summarize the three perspectives:

- **Perspective 1:** Behavioral reformation that occurs out of fear of going to hell if the behavior is not reformed.
- **Perspective 2:** Behavioral reformation that occurs out of the desire to earn right standing with God and access to heaven after death.

- **Perspective 3**: Behavioral reformation out of love and gratitude toward God because He gave us the gift of salvation through Jesus' finished work on the cross.

There you have it. Now, let's break it down. Perspectives 1 and 2 look different on the surface, but they are essentially the same motivators. Perspective 1 fuels lifestyle change out of fear of going to hell; Perspective 2 fuels lifestyle change out of the desire to go to heaven. Both lifestyle changes occur out of a desire to get God to give them what they want because of their good behavior. When it comes to a person's interactions with God, these first two perspectives wrongly suppose a person must be "good enough" to be saved from their sins. With this, it's not surprising the corporate fear of being rejected by God is a highly effective way to get a group of people to capitulate and obey. Sadly, these first two perspectives overlook that right standing with God is a gift that can only be obtained through faith in Jesus' finished work on the cross.

Now let's analyze Perspective 3—the perspective that fuels behavioral reformation the right way. Behavioral reformation in the church should occur out of heartfelt love and gratitude toward God for the gift of salvation He gave us through Jesus. The Bible teaches we are saved through trusting in Jesus' sin-cleansing work on the cross to make us right with God. When we trust in the Savior, we are freely saved, and this salvation has *absolutely nothing* to do with behavioral reformation. In fact, this salvation often happens to a person long before she has any behavioral improvements taking place in her life. It is by faith in Jesus that a person has her sins forgiven.

This is the Gospel according to the Bible. So when a person truly understands this good news, the natural result is she will often be motivated to live obediently toward God out of pure love and gratitude. It is as natural to respond this way as it would be if someone on earth unexpectedly gave us an expensive gift we didn't deserve and couldn't afford. We would be so blown away by this person's great kindness that our natural response would be to feel affection and adoration toward that person—and many of us would naturally return the kindness in whatever way we could.

CHANGING OUR BEHAVIOR GOD'S WAY

You can clearly see from one person to the next, the motivation fueling behavioral reformation can be very different. One person is motivated toward compliance to God's commandments out of *fear*—just as an ax raised above a person's neck would motivate obedience. Another person is motivated toward *willful* obedience through love, gratitude, and respect. What is motivating you to act and think like Jesus?

The Bible teaches that God loved us and sent Jesus to die for us while we were still sinners. We read:

> But God demonstrates His own love toward us, in that while we were still sinners, Christ died for us. Much more then, having now been justified by His blood, we shall be saved from wrath through Him.
> Romans 5:8–9, NKJV

Yes! It's true! God loved us while we were still sinners! Jesus died for us while we were still sinners! When sinners like us accept God's gift of salvation through trusting in Jesus' sin-cleansing death on the cross, God legally and officially releases us of all our guilt on the spot.

After we receive the gift of salvation, our appointment with hell is canceled, and we are handed our free ticket to heaven. With a ticket to heaven in our pocket and our receipt for hell in the wastebasket, fear is destroyed. From this point forward, it should be our love and gratitude toward our heavenly Father and Jesus our Savior that causes us to *want* to change our behavior. The fuel is love, not fear! The Bible says the Holy Spirit comes to live inside us after we believe and are forgiven, and He is constantly at work, teaching and helping us to reform our lives for the good of God.

Salvation always comes *before* true behavioral reformation. We can't even begin to truly reform ourselves until the Holy Spirit helps us, and salvation never depended on our good behavior anyway. Motivation free of fear and propelled by love is the type that pleases God. It teaches total and complete faith in Jesus alone for salvation, attributes all glory for our salvation to Him exclusively, and causes behavioral reformation out of love—not out of anxiety, terror, and self-interest. This is a change in behavior God's way! When we see this behavioral change happening in our churches, then we can know with certainty this is a genuine "movement of God."

Part 5

GOING EVEN DEEPER STILL

Chapter 17

ARE YOU SEEKING THE ALL-KNOWING, ONE-EYED SAGE?

HAVE YOU EVER stopped to honestly ask yourself, "Who is responsible for what I believe?" This is a tremendously important question, especially when we consider that you will either be (a) *saved* by believing the truth or (b) *spiritually lost* by falling for a lie. So who is that one person you can point your index finger at and declare, "You hold the ultimate responsibility to make sure I hear the truth"? As you answer this question, your finger better be turned around and pointing right back at yourself. The Bible has always taught that each of us is entirely responsible for his or her chosen beliefs. Are you taking your responsibility seriously?

THE PROBLEM WITH HUMAN LEADERS (INCLUDING ME)

I'm not sure where we got this crazy idea, but many of us thought someone else was responsible for making sure we knew the truth. Was this really a trustworthy belief to hold? We all know of some really fantastic authority figures who vocalize their opinions, yet who among us would ever imagine any leader or teacher could be correct 100 percent of the time? *Nobody* is correct all the time. I certainly am not. Spiritual influencers accumulate their theological ideas from many different sources, including their intellects, religious books, other leaders, religious TV shows, conferences, blogs and websites, professors, their childhood faith community (if they had one), family and friends, etc. Human inadequacy touches each of these sources. So what are we left with if our human leaders reference imperfect sources? We are left with imperfect leaders who sometimes teach us from imperfect sources. While many of these people have wonderful intentions, it is sensible for each of us to have a prudent awareness of the humanness of our teachers. I suppose this is the main problem with human leaders: They're human like we are.

LOOKING FOR THE ALL-KNOWING SAGE

Right about now you may be wondering, "If all my teachers are springs that pour out both truth and error, how will I know what is right from wrong? Who on earth can I trust in my search for the absolute truth—especially about the search for salvation?" These honest questions reveal the noble search for truth is taking place in your heart, but they also highlight an unhealthy craving to place ultimate trust in a fallible human being. Should we really lean so heavily upon a corn stalk?

Some of us remember those childhood adventure books and movies where the explorers scaled the rocky crags of a shadowy mountain, trying to reach the dark and cryptic temple. (And don't forget the lightning. There is always lightning!) Up on the mountaintop, they find that old, shrouded, one-eyed sage with the scratchy voice who can give them the answers to all the most enigmatic questions of the universe.

Just like these movies, some people in the real world imagine some religious figure out there who has the answers to all our deepest spiritual questions—maybe an author, pastor, professor, or itinerant preacher. But is this really true? Are there really mystical people out there who speak words that should be unquestionably accepted as Gospel truth? If you are looking for an all-knowing sage to believe in, then I guess I'll be the one to break it to you: That guy only exists in the movies.

WOULD GOD REALLY ALLOW A LEADER TO MISLEAD ME?

As we consider the human imperfections of our teachers and leaders, you might be wondering, "Would God really allow a leader to mislead me?" It is good you are wrestling with this topic, but this is the wrong question. God has made *you* the watchman at your gate, standing as the chief guard of your mind. You are in charge of which beliefs you let in and which you refuse and turn away. Nobody can ever force you to believe anything, so it makes sense to conclude you *choose* what you will believe. You are responsible— period. It doesn't stop here. Beyond receiving the God-given mission of guarding your mind against fallacy, you have also been given the responsibility of proactively seeking the truth for yourself. Yes, God expects you to seek His truth. There is no sympathy for the slothful. So with this said, we shouldn't ask, "Would God let a leader mislead me?" Instead, we should ask: "Would *I* let a leader mislead me?" We cannot shift responsibility. Each of us is responsible to proactively seek the truth for ourselves and vigilantly guard our minds against fallacy.

WOULD GOD REALLY HOLD ME RESPONSIBLE IF I BELIEVED A LIE?

If we were misguided through innocently trusting a faulty teacher, would God really hold you and me responsible? The answer to this question may be more serious than you think. Jesus noted that many religious authorities of His day were actually leading people away from salvation through offering them false teaching. He said to them: "Woe to you, teachers of the Law and Pharisees, you hypocrites! You shut the door of the kingdom of heaven in people's faces. You yourselves do not enter, nor will you let those enter who are trying to" (Matthew 23:13, NIV). Jesus called these trusted leaders "blind guides." Blind guides, huh? From what we read here, a leader can teach something so false it actually stops the trusting listeners from entering the kingdom of heaven—from joining God's family on earth and spending eternity with God in Heaven. False teaching *can* stop someone from being saved if they believe it. I can only imagine the shock of the unlucky fish as it takes the bait and gets dragged out of the pond with a hook in its lip.

SOME GOOD NEWS

Thankfully, God has given us two critically-important supports to help lead us to the truth we so desperately need: (1) the Holy Bible, and (2) the Holy Spirit. The Holy Bible has been the perfect wellspring of truth ever since God first instructed the prophets to put their quill to the papyrus thousands of years ago. The Bible is God's infallible words written in a book, and these words never fail us as human teachers do. When God declares or promises something, it is true and always happens. We can stand securely on God's Word, knowing it is a foundation that will never be shaken. This is where we find solid answers to all our most important questions—especially regarding the question about how we can obtain right standing with God.

God has also graciously sent His Holy Spirit—His glorious presence—to live inside every Christian believer. In biblical times, God's presence dwelled in a temple, but now it is as if each believer is a living, walking temple that the Spirit of God lives in. The Holy Spirit is a constant help to us, speaking quietly within our hearts, leading us to the answers to the most important spiritual questions we have. We learn to discern His voice with time. Interestingly enough, He often shows us these answers right as we are sitting down and searching for truth in the Scriptures.

Yes, the Holy Spirit and the Holy Bible are a power-packed duo straight from God, given to us because He loves us and wants us to find and grasp the truth. Every believer should ask the Holy Spirit for help with the questions they have, patiently waiting, believing He will bring them the answers in His perfect timing. The Holy Spirit even helps those who aren't yet saved find their way to the salvation Jesus offers them. The Holy Bible and the Holy Spirit are the two trustworthy, never-failing sources of truth we can count on.

THE PRIMARY SOURCE VS. SUPPLEMENTS

Now that we have established the authority of the teaching of the Holy Bible and Holy Spirit above all the teachings of man, we are ready to have a balanced look at God's awesome plan for His chosen human teachers. Although we are imperfect, God will often use true believers who are well versed in the Holy Scriptures to help other believers understand the truths of the Bible better. The Bible says the Holy Spirit has officially recruited certain people in the faith community to be Bible teachers, and these people can help others understand what the Scriptures are saying, often providing useful insight in the hard-to-understand areas of the text. These teachers can also teach us how to effectively study our Bibles in our daily lives. (See Ephesians 4:11–16 for more information on these God-gifted teachers)

Knowing no human being can teach us perfectly, it is always best to deliberately put the Bible first in our lives, and use teachers as supplements. I will say this again: It is always best to put the Bible first in our lives, using Bible teachers as *supplements*. The Bible should always be the main course, and the Bible teachers are the condiments. This goes for religious books as well. True Bible teachers are to be a help, but they are not to be the final say nor our main focus. Likewise, we should spend far more time reading the Holy Bible than reading religious books attempting to explain the Bible (for better or for worse). The Bible is always to be the final say, and the Holy Spirit always teaches what is seamlessly aligned with God's Word because the Holy Spirit is the Spirit of God Himself. The Bible is *His* book, so He is the only one able to explain it perfectly.

THREE SIGNS OF A GOOD TEACHER

Here are three signs of a good teacher: First, a good teacher will be more than willing to acknowledge his human fallibility as a teacher. This is true humility, and it acknowledges his need for the accountability of others and the constant help of the Holy Spirit. Second, a good teacher should feel comfortable when listeners test and judge his teaching by the standard of the Bible. In fact, a good teacher will encourage this! Third, a good teacher will always urge his listeners toward the infallible teaching of God's Word and toward the guidance of the Holy Spirit. He will deeply care about their welfare and desires they stay ever nearer to the two perfect Helpers God gave us.

FOLLOW THE EXAMPLE OF THE "NOBLE" BEREANS

We have a living example of truth seekers who tested their teacher and were honored in the Scriptures for doing so. This wise group of people was from the ancient city of Berea (located in modern-day Greece). These wise people judged the words of their famous teacher against the infallible Scriptures. You would not believe who they were judging: The apostle Paul! We read:

> As soon as it was night, the believers sent Paul and Silas away to Berea. On arriving there, they went to the Jewish synagogue. Now the Berean Jews were of more noble character than those in Thessalonica, for they received the message with great eagerness and examined the Scriptures every day to see if what Paul said was true.
> Acts 17:10–11, NIV

The Apostle Paul wrote at least thirteen of the twenty-seven books in the New Testament—that's approximately half the New Testament books and the people of Berea were using the Bible to check the words he said and were called "noble" for doing so. It was the principle of putting God's Word above man's that the Scriptures praised. From this passage, we learn two important things. First, it is good to have a ready mind to receive the truth from our teachers. Second, however, we should always hold out on swallowing their teaching until we thoroughly make sure it all aligns perfectly with the Holy Bible. If it all lines up, we can be sure there aren't any dangerous hooks hidden in there.

A FINAL CHALLENGE

We were never commanded to trust a man like we trust God—unless we are talking about Jesus. A perceptive mind will understand the teachings floating around out there come in all different types: good, bad, and everything in between. Even our most sincere leaders cannot lead and teach perfectly. With this said, it is wise for each of us to acknowledge God has placed the responsibility for searching for and discerning truth upon our shoulders—not on the shoulders of someone else. We should each take that responsibility seriously, using the help God has given us through the Holy Bible and the Holy Spirit. Studying the Bible should be a daily discipline, and relying on the Holy Spirit's guidance should be a moment-by-moment practice. Let us have ready ears and open hearts as we listen to the leaders and teachers before us, but let us never neglect to check their teachings with the words of the Scriptures and the voice of the Holy Spirit. If we learn to lean on God's two great Companions, we will not falter—and this is especially relevant in Gospel teaching.

Chapter 18

WHAT ABOUT THOSE WHO HAVE NEVER HEARD ABOUT JESUS? (MIRACLES OF MERCY)

I S IT POSSIBLE for someone to be saved if they have never heard about and believed in Jesus? This is a common question and one with which many of us wrestle. Fortunately, God's Word is thorough, and every critical question we could surface is answered either directly or indirectly somewhere in there.

In the book of Acts, God allows us to see a textbook case study of a man who had never heard about Jesus and all He had accomplished on the cross. This wonderful, God-ordained story in the center of Acts effectively communicates an answer to the difficult question above.

A DEVOUT, RELIGIOUS PERSON WHO IS NOT SAVED

The New Testament retells the interesting story of a man named Cornelius, and this event took place shortly after Jesus' death, resurrection, and ascension into heaven. Cornelius was "a devout,

God-fearing man, as was everyone in his household. He gave generously to the poor and prayed regularly to God" (Acts 10:2, NLT). Morally speaking, we see Cornelius was an ethical person, devoted to upright behavior, and deeply committed to helping the poor. We also see he believed in God the Creator and prayed to Him regularly. Here is where we ask: Was the virtuous, giving, and prayerful Cornelius saved and reconciled to God even though he had never heard about the saving message of Jesus? The Bible's clear answer is: *No!* Cornelius was not saved before coming to know of Jesus. Let's discover why this is so by studying the story a little closer. God sent an angel to Cornelius and told him to send for Peter. Why was Peter to be summoned? The angel explained that Peter would "bring you a message through which you and all your household will be saved" (Acts 11:14, NIV). Here we see, despite all the wonderful things Cornelius had going for him, he still needed more to be saved—he needed *Jesus*. Peter knew the soul-saving message about Jesus, but Cornelius didn't, so these two guys needed to get together and have a conversation. Next, we see the Holy Spirit *did not* come upon Cornelius before he knew about Jesus, even though he was a man of prayer and good works. However, as soon as Peter told him about Jesus' death and resurrection and how a person's sins can be forgiven through Him, Cornelius believed the message and the Holy Spirit filled him immediately. This is exactly how it was reported in the book of Acts. (See Acts 10:34–44)

GOOD INTENTIONS NOT ENOUGH

Good behavior, giving to the poor, religious devotion, good motives, belief in God, and prayers to the Creator will not save you from the consequences of your sins on judgment day. If we take the Bible's examples for our instruction, we find it is only by hearing and believing the Gospel message that a person can be made right with God. Our sins can only be forgiven by hearing and believing Jesus bore our sins in our place. Why? Because God sent the Savior to take all our punishment for our sins upon Himself. This is God's path, and we must follow it. Once we believe, God gives us the gift of the Holy Spirit as internal proof we have been saved!

GOD'S MIRACLES OF MERCY

One important thing to remember about Cornelius is God noticed his prayers and good works, for the angel said: "Your prayers and gifts to the poor have been received by God as an offering!" (Acts 10:4, NLT) While some people feel uncomfortable with the idea that people who have not heard about Jesus could be inevitably lost in their sins and remain unsaved, we must look at this amazing case study and remember what we see: *God is actively looking around the planet and doing miracles of mercy to bring the Gospel to those who are seeking truth.* This is evidence for God's great love and mercy, and who among us really knows how incredibly often these miracles of mercy are taking place around the jungles, deserts, and cities of the world! To further state His case, in three consecutive chapters in the book of Acts, God has given us amazing examples of ways He has sought out people, assuring they would hear the Gospel of Jesus and be saved. (See Acts 8:26–40, Acts 9:1–19, and Acts 10)

— Chapter 19 —

5 DIFFICULT BIBLE PASSAGES EXPLAINED

MOST OF THE Bible's teachings about God's salvation message are extremely clear, and we should thank God for this. Sadly, there have been a small handful of Bible passages that certain wayward teachers have routinely taken out of context. These teachers are headed down the wrong path, and many of them desire for others to follow their lead. We must equip ourselves to discern where these teachings go awry, and in doing so, protect the biblical understanding of the Gospel in our minds and the minds of others around us.

We will deal with five of the most commonly misrepresented biblical passages. To find the correct interpretation, we want to ask ourselves: "What was the author or speaker trying to communicate to the original listeners?" To answer this question, it is important to determine the context of the verse (what comes before and after the verse in focus). You will soon see by checking the context of these excellent but oft-misused passages, the true meaning will quickly become apparent. I am now calling on readers to give their full attention because this analysis will require us to fully engage the brains God has given us. Here we go!

DIFFICULT PASSAGE #1:
HEBREWS 10:26–31

HEBREWS 10:26–31 SAYS: "If we deliberately keep on sinning after we have received the knowledge of the truth, no sacrifice for sins is left, but only a fearful expectation of judgment and of raging fire that will consume the enemies of God. Anyone who rejected the law of Moses died without mercy on the testimony of two or three witnesses. How much more severely do you think someone deserves to be punished who has trampled the Son of God underfoot, who has treated as an unholy thing the blood of the covenant that sanctified them, and who has insulted the Spirit of grace? For we know Him who said, 'It is mine to avenge; I will repay,' and again, 'The Lord will judge His people.' It is a dreadful thing to fall into the hands of the living God" (NIV).

FALSE TEACHERS LIKE TO SAY: "Believers beware: If you deliberately do the same sin repeatedly after you come to faith in Jesus, you will lose your salvation. Jesus' sacrificial death will not save you if you do this. Then, it is not by faith alone that Jesus saves you, but your works of obedience and refraining from sin also plays a part. With this said, believers must be careful to be obedient to all God's commandments, or we may end up losing our salvation."

GOD'S INTENDED INTERPRETATION: Context matters here! The major thrust of the book of Hebrews is to encourage persecuted Jewish people who believe in Jesus not to reject Jesus by committing a very particular sin: *The Sin of Unbelief.* Hebrews 2:1–4 summarizes the primary theme of the whole book:

> We must pay the most careful attention, therefore, to what
> we have heard, so that we do not drift away. For since the

message spoken through angels was binding, and every violation and disobedience received its just punishment, how shall we escape if we ignore so great a salvation? This salvation, which was first announced by the Lord, was confirmed to us by those who heard Him. God also testified to it by signs, wonders and various miracles, and by gifts of the Holy Spirit distributed according to His will. (NIV)

Chapter 2 is encouraging the readers "so that we do not drift away" from faith in Jesus. Chapters 3 and 4 continue developing this theme by speaking about the Israelites committing the same sin— The Sin of Unbelief—while they were wandering in the wilderness after miraculously escaping slavery in Egypt. We read:

See to it, brothers and sisters, that none of you has a sinful, unbelieving heart that turns away from the living God. But encourage one another daily, as long as it is called 'Today,' so that none of you may be hardened by sin's deceitfulness. We have come to share in Christ, if indeed we hold our original conviction firmly to the very end. As has just been said: 'Today, if you hear His voice, do not harden your hearts as you did in the rebellion."

Who were they who heard and rebelled? Were they not all those Moses led out of Egypt? And with whom was he angry for forty years? Was it not with those who sinned, whose bodies perished in the wilderness? And to whom did God swear that they would never enter his rest if not to those who disobeyed? So we see that they were not able to enter, because of their unbelief. Hebrews 3:12–19, NIV

Even though the Israelites were freed from slavery and on their way to a place of rest in the Promised Land, they died in the desert along the way due to their *sin of unbelief*. Chapter 4 continues the thought: "God's promise of entering his rest still stands, so we ought to tremble with fear that some of you might fail to experience it. For this good news—that God has prepared this rest—has been announced to us just as it was to them. But it did them no good because they didn't share the faith of those who listened to God" (Hebrews 4:1–2, NLT). The book of Hebrews is teaching us that just like the generation of Israelites who failed to reach their earthly Promised Land because of their unbelief, so we too will fail to reach our Promised Land of heaven if we fall into the sin of unbelief. Despite being initially saved by faith, a person could fall between their moment of faith and the time they reached heaven—*if* they stopped believing in Jesus.

As we come up to the tricky verses of Hebrews 10:26–31, we must remember to consider the context, reading both *before* and *after* this passage. If we do this, thinking about the verse in light of its context, we recognize the specific sin referred to in Hebrews 10 is *the sin of unbelief in Jesus*. Again, it says: "If we deliberately keep on sinning after we have received the knowledge of the truth, no sacrifice for sins is left, but only a fearful expectation of judgment and of raging fire that will consume the enemies of God" (Hebrews 10:26–27, NIV). This can be a terrifying verse for believers if we forget the context. We all sin, and sometimes our sin is *deliberate*. If we keep everything in context, we notice the passage before it states: "Let us hold fast the confession of our hope without wavering, for He who promised is faithful" (Hebrews 10:23, ESV). This means the author is urging believers to continue proclaiming their faith in Jesus without wavering and hanging on to the hope of our salvation even under the trials of great persecution. If we check the context afterward, we see the theme continues: "Therefore do not cast away your confidence, which has great reward....But we are not of those who draw back to perdition, but of those who believe to the saving of the soul" (Hebrews 10:35, 10:39, NKJV).

The entire next chapter, Hebrews 11, is referred to as "The Hall of Faith," and it states that "without faith it is impossible to please God..." (Hebrews 11:6). Chapter 11 points to a long list of people who held on to their faith firmly to the end, never giving up, even as many of them faced death rather than quit trusting in Jesus as their Savior. Speaking of these intense persecutions these wonderful people of faith endured through, we read:

> But others were tortured, refusing to turn from God in order to be set free. They placed their hope in a better life after the resurrection. Some were jeered at, and their backs were cut open with whips. Others were chained in prisons. Some died by stoning, some were sawed in half, and others were killed with the sword. Some went about wearing skins of sheep and goats, destitute and oppressed and mistreated. They were too good for this world, wandering over deserts and mountains, hiding in caves and holes in the ground. All these people earned a good reputation because of their faith...
> Hebrews 11:35–39, NLT

After checking the context as good Bible readers do, we see a careful reading of Hebrews 10:26–31 shows this does not claim a believer in Jesus who willfully commits any random sin will not be forgiven and will certainly go to hell. Far from it! Instead, it teaches that those who have known the truth of the Gospel yet choose to deliberately reject faith in the Savior are rejecting Him and the sin-atoning blood He shed for us. This person cannot be saved, for there is no salvation apart from the Savior, Jesus. The author wants us to stand strong and unwavering in our faith.

DIFFICULT PASSAGE #2:
MATTHEW 5:20

MATTHEW 5:20 SAYS: "For I tell you that unless your righteousness surpasses that of the Pharisees and the teachers of the law, you will certainly not enter the kingdom of heaven" (NIV).

FALSE TEACHERS LIKE TO SAY: "Salvation by faith in Jesus is certainly not enough to get into heaven. Jesus is good and helpful, but people must also *behave* their way to be saved. Jesus said in Matthew 5:20 that we must behave extremely righteous to get into heaven—so good that it even surpasses the religious leaders of Jesus' day. Salvation comes by behaving righteous enough to enter the kingdom of heaven."

GOD'S INTENDED INTERPRETATION: The Bible is clear that salvation is a gift not dependent on our works. The wonderful gifts of God: forgiveness, reconciliation, and a place in heaven don't depend on the goodness of our behavior, but on God's. Salvation comes to us by faith despite our shortcomings. Thank God! This means believers can have perfect assurance of salvation as we trust in Jesus to save us from our sin guilt. The Bible says: "For it is by grace you have been saved, through faith—and this is not from yourselves, it is the gift of God—not by works, so that no one can boast" (Ephesians 2:8–9, NIV).

After considering the teachings of Ephesians 2:8–9 and knowing Scripture will not contradict itself, we see there must be a better, more accurate interpretation for Matthew 5:20. A better interpretation aligns perfectly with the doctrine of salvation by faith. Jesus was talking to His disciples who all believed the Pharisees and Scribes were the most obedient, law-abiding people on the planet.

The disciples wrongly believed if anyone would get to heaven, it would certainly be the Pharisees and Scribes, for they really worked hard to obey God's laws. But Jesus said even obeying God's law really, really well was *not* enough to get a person into heaven.

Jesus knew that to get to heaven a person must not only be better than the Pharisees, but he must be absolutely PERFECT. James 2:10 describes God's standard of perfection: "For whoever keeps the whole law and yet stumbles at just one point is guilty of breaking all of it" (James 2:10, NIV). What Jesus was trying to teach His disciples in Matthew 5:20 is nobody can ever work their way into heaven by being good; instead, they must receive total forgiveness by believing in the Savior who would take the punishment for all their sins.

Jesus made this clear: "For God so loved the world that He gave His one and only Son, that whoever believes in Him shall not perish but have eternal life. For God did not send His Son into the world to condemn the world, but to save the world through Him. Whoever believes in Him is not condemned, but whoever does not believe stands condemned already because they have not believed in the name of God's one and only Son" (John 3:16–18, NIV). Jesus was all about salvation by faith.

DIFFICULT PASSAGE #3:
MATTHEW 16:24–25

MATTHEW 16:24–25 SAYS: "Then Jesus said to His disciples, 'Whoever wants to be my disciple must deny themselves and take up their cross and follow me. For whoever wants to save their life will lose it, but whoever loses their life for me will find it.'" (NIV)

FALSE TEACHERS LIKE TO SAY: "Jesus taught in Matthew 16:24–25 that if you want to be His disciple and be saved, you must take up your cross and crucify your sinful nature with all its wrong desires. This means if you do not totally deny the sinful desires in you, then you will not be saved."

GOD'S INTENDED INTERPRETATION: The disciples had expected Jesus to soon become a mighty king over Israel—an earthly ruler with great prestige and power. Because they had been faithfully following Jesus since the beginning of His public ministry, they believed they would be raised into significant positions of power and wealth when Jesus finally took His place on the throne over Israel. This was very misled considering the humble purpose for Jesus' first coming.

Jesus was not suggesting His disciples would have to "crucify their sinful natures" enough if they wanted to be saved—as some false teachers advocate. Yes, Jesus wants us to stop sinning, but this verse really has nothing to do with that at all. In this passage, Jesus was pointing out to His disciples that if they wanted to follow Him, they would have to be ready to receive extreme persecution. In fact, following Him would be a lot more uncomfortable than they ever thought.

Look back a few verses to Matthew 16:21–23 where Jesus was telling His disciples He would soon end up suffering and dying in Jerusalem. Peter and the other disciples did not believe Jesus would suffer and die; instead, they thought He would soon be honored and exalted as king over all the earth. Jesus let them know they would have to experience intense persecution—even death—if they were going to walk by His side and be His disciples. They were to follow Jesus even if they had to be crucified for their faith. Interestingly enough, Peter was eventually crucified in Rome for his faith in Jesus. With this said, we should always remember salvation comes by simple faith in the Savior. It is God's gift to those who receive it freely, and no amount of self-purification is involved in receiving it.

DIFFICULT PASSAGE #4:
PHILIPPIANS 2:12

PHILIPPIANS 2:12 SAYS: "Therefore, my dear friends, as you have always obeyed—not only in my presence, but now much more in my absence—continue to work out your salvation with fear and trembling" (NIV).

FALSE TEACHERS LIKE TO SAY: "This verse teaches if you want to have salvation, you will need to 'work out your salvation' by doing many good things and refraining from doing bad things. Your eternal destiny is on the line. If you fail to live up to God's standard of obedience, you will go to hell—whether you believe in Jesus. So you should continue to strive to be good enough for God, and do so with fear and trembling. After all, you don't want to go to hell, do you?"

GOD'S INTENDED INTERPRETATION: Contrary to the unbiblical interpretations of false teachers, this passage is talking about standing firm in faith through persecution—holding onto faith even through fear and trembling that comes when looking death in the face. How do we know Paul is talking about persecution here? By checking the *context*. Context matters, and without checking the context we lose the true meaning and make ourselves vulnerable to inaccurate interpretation.

First, we learn earlier (in Philippians 1:13) that Paul is writing from chains in prison in Rome, under persecution for his faith. Second, looking for the context of Philippians 2:12, we read the following a handful of verses before: "Whatever happens, conduct yourselves in a manner worthy of the gospel of Christ. Then, whether I come and see you or only hear about you in my absence, I will know that you stand firm in the one Spirit, striving together as one for the faith of the gospel without being frightened in any way by those who oppose you. This is a sign to them that they will be destroyed, but that you will be saved—and that by God. For it has been granted to you on behalf of Christ not only to believe in Him, but also to suffer for Him, since you are going through the same struggle you saw I had, and now hear that I still have" (Philippians 1:27–30, NIV). This thought then logically leads Paul to encourage the believers to "continue to work out your salvation with fear and trembling." The believers were being called to persevere in faith even though they would likely face terrifying trials and have to persevere through fearful trembling. If they continued to hold on to their faith in Jesus for their salvation, they would be saved.

DIFFICULT PASSAGE #5:
JAMES 2:18–26

JAMES 2:18–26 SAYS: "But someone may well say, 'You have faith and I have works; show me your faith without the works, and I will show you my faith by my works.' You believe that God is one. You do well; the demons also believe, and shudder. But are you willing to recognize, you foolish fellow, that faith without works is useless? Was not Abraham our father justified by works when he offered up Isaac his son on the altar? You see that faith was working with his works, and as a result of the works, faith was perfected; and the Scripture was fulfilled which says, 'And Abraham believed God, and it was reckoned to him as righteousness,' and he was called the friend of God. You see that a man is justified by works and not by faith alone. In the same way, was not Rahab the harlot also justified by works when she received the messengers and sent them out by another way? For just as the body without the spirit is dead, so also faith without works is dead" (NASB).

FALSE TEACHERS LIKE TO SAY: "Yes, we know Jesus matters to our salvation. But faith in Jesus is not enough: We need more. James taught we must also have works if we want to be saved. So we need Jesus plus strict obedience to God's laws and commandments if we want to make it into heaven."

GOD'S INTENDED INTERPRETATION: Faith saves us, and not our works. As we saw earlier, Ephesians 2:8–9 says: "For it is by grace you have been saved, through faith—and this is not from yourselves, it is the gift of God—not by works, so that no one can boast" (NIV). Galatians 2:16 agrees with this point, and it says: "Yet we know that a person is made right with God by faith in Jesus Christ, not by obeying the law. And we have believed in Christ Jesus, so that we might be made right with God because of our faith in Christ, not because we have obeyed the law. For no one will ever be made right with God by obeying the law" (NLT). Nobody can be made right with God by obeying God's law; instead, they must be made right with God through faith in Jesus and His finished work on the cross.

So what is the correct interpretation of this James passage? James 2:18–26 tells us that when someone truly believes in Jesus, you can tell that faith is inside by the actions on the outside. You know a teapot is boiling on the inside when you outwardly hear the sounds it makes and see the steam pouring out. Similarly, you know faith has come alive in a person when you see some change happening on the outside—yet it is certainly not the outward change that saves him or her in any way.

Another thing we should not forget is the two examples James gave us of Abraham and Rahab do not in any way suggest they were doing "good works" as we might usually think of them. Let's look at each situation. First, Abraham knew God had promised his son, Isaac, would become his heir, but this could not happen if Isaac died before Abraham. So when God tested Abraham by telling him to sacrifice Isaac, Abraham had no problem following through because he knew God could be trusted. Somehow, some way, God would fulfill His promise to allow Isaac to be Abraham's heir—even if God had to resurrect Isaac from the dead. By Abraham going to nearly sacrificing Isaac, it proved Abraham really trusted God and had faith on the inside. Note this was not any activity one would usually think would fall into the category of "good works."

The second examples of "works" that prove faith was the case of Rahab. Rahab was raised in a pagan nation, and she lived in the large fortress city of Jericho that stood in the Israelites path between Egypt and the Promised Land. Although it may have seemed the massive city walls she lived in were impenetrable, Rahab had heard about the God of Israel, and had believed in Him so much that she knew in her heart He would certainly help the Israelites overtake her evil city. So because of her faith, she betrayed her city and helped the Israelites overcome her people. She had faith in the God of Israel on the inside, and it was not surprising her actions on the outside aligned logically with that inner faith.

In both the cases of Abraham and Rahab, they were doing outward actions that revealed they truly believed in God. James is saying this should be the same for us as believers: A believer should and will show outward evidence of inward faith. It happens naturally—it's just the way it works. However, the Scriptures make it clear that our outward works cannot do a thing to save us because doing good things and refraining from bad things can never remove our past guilt and cleanse our conscience from past sins. Only faith in the Savior can cleanse us of sin and make us right with God, so we should always continue to recognize we are saved by faith and not by works.

CONCLUSION

The enemy of our souls will always try to get us to misinterpret Scripture. Satan even used this trick of misinterpretation on Jesus when he tempted Him to sin. Jesus didn't fall for the enemy's crafty tricks, and we shouldn't either. We must always remember we should add nothing to salvation by simple faith in Jesus, and to carefully check the context of each Scripture we read—especially verses that impact our view on salvation. If we do this, we'll be secure in our faith, and ready to defeat the lies the enemy throws our way.

— *Chapter 20* —

"ASK JESUS INTO YOUR HEART"?

Taking the twelve disciples aside, Jesus said, "Listen, we're going up to Jerusalem, where all the predictions of the prophets concerning the Son of Man will come true. He will be handed over to the Romans, and he will be mocked, treated shamefully, and spit upon. They will flog him with a whip and kill him, but on the third day he will rise again."
Luke 18:31–33, NLT

I N MY MIND'S EYE, I can see a young father and mother speaking with their seven-year-old child, trying to delicately explain how a person can be saved. As loving coaches, they provide the following instruction: "All you have to do is ask Jesus to live inside your heart, and you can go to heaven someday." Many reading this book may have found themselves in a similar situation. Trying to explain the Gospel for little ears can be a challenge. But one thing we can be sure of: Regardless of noble intentions, telling a child they are saved by asking Jesus to come "live inside your heart" is an oversimplification of the Gospel that really does a disservice to the little listener.

INCOMPLETE PERSPECTIVES OF SALVATION

There are countless perspectives people use to think about Jesus and salvation—some perspectives are *correct*, some are *incorrect*, and some are *incomplete*. Let's look at several insufficient ways of thinking about Jesus. Each of the following statements express an *incomplete* understanding of the Savior and His Gospel:

- **INCOMPLETE:** "Jesus was just another prophet in the lineup of many prophets."
- **INCOMPLETE:** "Jesus was a moral figure sent by God to show us how to live right."
- **INCOMPLETE:** "You must acknowledge Jesus' historical existence to be saved."
- **INCOMPLETE:** "We can be saved by asking God for forgiveness."
- **INCOMPLETE:** "God loves us, and therefore He forgives us when we ask Him."

As you can see from this list above, not all things "Jesus" are actually of Jesus, and not all Gospel presentations are complete and able to save. With this thought now established, let us make sure we do not withhold any important Gospel details God has given us. To believe you must only "ask Jesus to come into your heart" to be saved is a seemingly innocent perspective, but like earlier examples, it is also an altogether *incomplete* perspective unable to save. What is the "Gospel" without a cross? To remove the cross from the Gospel message is to remove all rationality from the message. If we tell a child that all we have to do is ask Jesus to "come into our hearts" to be saved, then the following question may soon follow:

"Why didn't God just rescue baby Jesus out of the manger and take Him to heaven, institute the 'ask Jesus into your heart' model of salvation, and save Jesus from the massive inconvenience of death on a wooden cross?"

It's easy to talk a child out of believing in Santa Claus, the Easter Bunny, and the Tooth Fairy once they hit a certain age. Let's not give our children another fairy tale to eventually grow out of.

What could even be worse is children may believe they have received all they need due to "asking Jesus in their hearts," and this false security might stop them from searching out the real Gospel when they get older. After all, why should they look for salvation through the cross when they already "asked Jesus into their hearts"?

THE CHILDREN OF ANCIENT ISRAEL

Let us all be very careful with how we present the Gospel message to children. The saving power of the Gospel message is nullified if Jesus' essential work on the cross is left out of it. No person can get to God without going the way of the cross of Jesus—not even the cute little sinners among us who still play on the swing set in the backyard.

Many children of ancient Israel deeply understood the connection between sin removal and animal sacrifice at the Jewish Temple in Jerusalem, and today we can also thoughtfully communicate the sacrificial work of Jesus to children and adult truth-seekers alike. Remember, the Gospel is extraordinarily simple. Be careful to preserve the integrity of the full Gospel by keeping the cross of Jesus central in every presentation of this amazing message.

Chapter 21

THE SURVEY REVEALS:
DANGEROUS DISTORTIONS OF THE GOSPEL

I ONCE HAD THE incredible opportunity to survey a large group of religious people, and I asked them how they would describe the "Gospel—God's message regarding how a person can obtain salvation." The crowd filled out questionnaires, and after receiving the results, I sat down and read each response, one after another. I found a handful of biblical Gospel descriptions in the survey results—some refined and some simple—and my heart was elated to see God had led many of these people to the truth. Yet this chapter has been written as a response to the significant number of survey answers that dangerously missed the mark. While looking at the survey responses, I was troubled the enemy of our souls has been incredibly busy creating and flooding the market with counterfeit "gospels." His aim, as always, is to keep humans away from the one saving truth.

In this chapter, I will identify a list of the dangerous Gospel distortions that came out of the survey results, and then I will give a biblical answer that diagnoses and corrects the error. You may find some survey responses bizarre and may scarcely believe they are real, yet they are real, and this is clear evidence we must diligently study the Gospel through the Bible's safety and guidance. The goal here is to help preserve the integrity of the Gospel message we believe and teach, keeping us safe on God's path to salvation.

DISTORTION #1

"Jesus died as a ransom to the devil, to purchase us back from the devil."

ANSWER: This statement has some *symbolic* truth to it, but it is technically not an accurate statement. The reality is our sin brought us trouble with *God.* In man's judicial system, one is in charge of judging and another is in charge of enforcing the penalty. In heaven's judicial system, God is in charge of the judgment against sin *and* the enforcement of the penalty. Our sin separated us from a relationship with a holy God; caused us to have guilt in God's heavenly judicial system; and assured us we would ultimately fail and be condemned on judgment day when we stand before God. With all this said, Jesus' so-called "ransom" of taking on our punishment was to God who we had sinned against, not to the devil. First Timothy 2:5–6 states: "There is one God and one mediator between God and mankind—the man Christ Jesus, who gave himself as a ransom for all people." (NIV). Jesus appeased the wrath of God against sinners through His sacrificial work on the cross. He is the Mediator between God and mankind.

DISTORTION #2

"We are saved because Jesus was raised from the dead for our justification."

ANSWER: The word "justification" means *the act of declaring or making a person right in God's sight.* What is it exactly that makes us right in God's sight? Let's be clear: It is not the resurrection of Jesus that makes us right in God's sight. Our sins are forgiven through Jesus' work on the cross—not through His resurrection. Jesus' *death* dealt with our sin issue once and for all, and Jesus' marvelous resurrection proves He really bore God's wrath for our sins when He died.

Any cult leader can say they are dying for the sins of humanity; however, we can justifiably believe Jesus really died for our sins when we see He resurrected from the dead. Only God has power over death, and Jesus' resurrection is the proof God had ordained His death and our sins were actually dealt with through that death. His sacrificial *death* gave us the ability to stand guilt-free before the judgment seat of God. The Bible tells us: "And since we have been made right in God's sight by the blood of Christ, he will certainly save us from God's condemnation" (Romans 5:9, NLT). What did this passage say? It said we were made right in God's sight through nothing other than the blood Jesus shed when He died while taking the punishment we deserved.

DISTORTION #3

"The sin atonement provided by Jesus is not enough to save us."

ANSWER: The previous statement is simply not true. Jesus' work on the cross was enough to cleanse us from all our sins and completely reconcile our relationship with God. He took the full punishment for our sins so that we don't have to, and those who trust in Jesus' atonement will be guilt-free on judgment day and will have a place in heaven. The Bible says:

> And since we have been made right in God's sight by the blood of Christ, he will certainly save us from God's condemnation. For since our friendship with God was restored by the death of his Son while we were still his enemies, we will certainly be saved through the life of his Son.
> Romans 5:9–10, NLT

This verse clearly points out we are friends with God—with nothing separating us from Him—all because Jesus' sin-atoning work on the cross was sufficient to save us.

DISTORTION #4

"Jesus' sin-atoning death is not enough to save us. We must also have the many righteous acts He accomplished while on earth credited to our account."

ANSWER: This is a fairly prevalent Gospel distortion, and it twists the truth, using something inherently true and good to teach something subtly deceptive. It is true Jesus performed many good works during His time on earth, and He is a perfect model of behavior because of this. But these good works do not help to save us, and we do not need good works "credited to our account" (Note: If you have never heard this teaching you might find it strange).

It was through Jesus' death on the cross that He took the guilt of our sins upon Himself and was fully punished in our place. The removal of sin makes us *righteous* in God's sight. Without the guilt of sin, there is nothing to separate us from God, and nothing to keep us out of heaven.

Right before Jesus died while hanging on the wooden cross, He triumphantly shouted out: "It is finished" (John 19:30, NIV)! The mountain of guilt that stood against sinners like you and me was completely dealt with, and Jesus' mission was accomplished as He expired while hanging up above. It was finished *at His death*. The apostle Paul explained:

> Now, brothers and sisters, I want to remind you of the gospel I preached to you, which you received and on which you have taken your stand. By this gospel you are saved, if you hold firmly to the word I preached to you. Otherwise, you have believed in vain. For what I received I passed on to you as of first importance: that Christ died for our sins according to the Scriptures, that he was buried, that he was raised on the third day according to the Scriptures.
> 1 Corinthians 15:1–4, NIV

We see the Gospel the apostle Paul preached said nothing about adding to Jesus' good work above and beyond the atonement for sin that He won for us at the cross. Instead, we see the good news focuses on "Christ died for our sins," and this is the good news. In Acts 10, while telling Cornelius the good news, Peter says nothing about the good works of Jesus needing to be credited to our records to be saved. Instead, we see the true Gospel declared: "All the prophets testify about him that everyone who believes in him receives forgiveness of sins through his name" (Acts 10:43, NIV). It is important to note Cornelius received salvation through putting his faith in the One who earned forgiveness of sins for him, and that was enough. Thankfully, this man never heard the fallacy we must have anything more than faith in Jesus to be saved.

After receiving complete forgiveness of sins through faith in Jesus' work on the cross, we need nothing extra because we stand faultless before God. Let's not confuse the issue by stating we need something more. Be very careful with this dangerous Gospel distortion because it has no scriptural anchor, so it is taught without God's authority.

DISTORTION #5

"We're saved by grace.
Grace is enough.
And faith too."

ANSWER: Many of us are familiar with the famous Bible verse: "It is by grace you have been saved through faith" (Ephesians 2:8). In this passage, the popular religious terms *grace* and *faith* are used. The word *grace* means *"unmerited gift"*; the word faith means *belief* or *trust*.

I once heard someone talking about how we have been "saved by grace through faith," yet this teacher never really talked about Jesus or what He did for us on the cross. It eventually came out the so-called "grace" he was referring to was not really anchored to Jesus; instead, the term "grace" was a random, abstract force that supposedly saved us. He also spoke about "faith," but he never anchored this to the historical event where Jesus our Savior dealt with our sin debt.

This is how I discovered an important discernment principle: just because a person uses religious words doesn't mean he is using the correct meaning behind those words. So if someone ever says, "I believe we are saved by faith," we should ask him exactly what he believes we must have faith in. If someone else says, "I believe we are saved by God's grace," we should ask him how God showed us His Grace. God's answer to both questions is "Jesus."

"Grace" means nothing apart from Jesus because through His work on the cross we receive God's unmerited favor. "Faith" means nothing apart from Jesus because without Him there would be no object of focus for our faith. We are not saved by some abstract, mystical thing we call "grace," but through God's unmerited gift given to us in Jesus' sacrificial work. We are not saved by "faith" in and of itself, but by directing our faith toward Jesus and all He accomplished for us on the cross. The words "grace" and "faith" really find their depth of meaning when we anchor them firmly to Jesus and His sin-cleansing work.

DISTORTION #6

"A person can be saved by accepting the spirit of Christ [without believing and accepting the historical death and resurrection of Jesus]."

ANSWER: What does this even mean? If we inquire of the Bible, we do not see any New Testament examples of people being saved without believing and accepting the historical death and resurrection of Jesus—the true Jesus and all He did for us. Consider the story of Cornelius as an example of this. Cornelius was "a devout, God-fearing man, as was everyone in his household. He gave generously to the poor and prayed regularly to God" (Acts 10:2, NLT). We see God recognized this man's good works and his prayers and alms (Acts 10:4). However, despite the notable goodness of Cornelius before hearing the Gospel message, an angel told him: "Send messengers to Joppa, and summon a man named Simon Peter. He will tell you how you and everyone in your household can be saved" (Acts 11:13–14, NLT). With this, Cornelius *did not* receive salvation from his sins nor did he receive the Holy Spirit until (a) he audibly heard the message of the historical death and resurrection of Jesus and (b) believed what he heard (Acts 10:39-47; Acts 11:14–15).

Do we really need to believe in Jesus' sacrificial death and resurrection to be saved? If we value the Bible's case study in Cornelius' life, then it looks like God requires a person to believe these things to be saved. Salvation is activated when we believe in the historical message of Jesus' sin-atoning death and the proof of its effectiveness as evidenced by His resurrection. With this said, believing in only "the spirit of Christ" without believing in the flesh and blood Jesus who came to give His true life for us is not the real Gospel.

DISTORTION #7

"A person is saved if they believe in Jesus."

ANSWER: This is great, but we must make sure we believe the whole story of Jesus. For example, just believing Jesus existed as a person is not sufficient; furthermore, believing He was just another prophet will not suffice. We must specifically believe Jesus was the Savior God sent to die in place of sinners, taking the full punishment for our sins so that we don't have to; we must also believe He came resurrected from the dead, proving He was the one true Savior. We need to believe and accept the full story of Jesus, adding nothing inaccurate to it, and we should tell the whole story when we share the Gospel with others. Saying that a person is saved "if they believe in Jesus" is correct, but we should make sure the person believes the right things about Jesus so that he or she can be saved.

DISTORTION #8

"We are saved by being faithful to God. Faith equals faithfulness. Our behavior must be faithful."

ANSWER: When the Bible says we are "saved by faith," God intends this to communicate we can be saved by belief in Jesus and His sin-atoning work for us. We are called to trust what He did for us is what saves us.

When someone says *faith* equals *faithfulness*, they are wrongly attributing an incorrect meaning to the word *faith*. If *faith* were the same as *faithfulness*, then we would have to obey to be saved, and the Bible makes it very clear this is not at all the case. If we are "saved by faith" and *faith* means *faithfulness*, then we would all be required to work hard for salvation by obeying God's law—something the Bible says nobody can do. We cannot obey to be saved. Nobody can be saved by their faithfulness. It is Jesus' faithfulness to go to the cross for us that paved the way for our salvation, and all we must do is to believe/trust in this wonderful Savior.

Chapter 22

WHAT TO DO WHEN LEADERS LEAD ASTRAY

I T IS DIFFICULT for us to accept the possibility that those we love and trust could ever be guilty of leading us astray from the *Gospel*—the area that matters most. In the history of the Gospel, many believers have sadly discovered that their leaders were teaching false gospels. Today, this could be a friend, a teacher, a parent, an author, a radio host, a television preacher, or even a pastor.

While we hope we never discover this in our leaders, it is not beyond possibility, and it's good to at least be prepared with principles for dealing with the situation if it arose. What should we do if we discover one of our influencers teaches a false gospel? How complex and emotionally difficult this situation would be. Should we continue to allow these leaders to influence us, or should we completely separate ourselves from their teaching? After all, a little poison in a 99 percent pure glass of water is definitely something to be concerned about.

THE AUTHOR'S OPINION

I feel very uncomfortable giving a person spiritual influence in my life when I discover they teach a false gospel. Jesus said: "For what will it profit a man if he gains the whole world and forfeits his soul?" (Matthew 16:26, ESV) If a fantastic teacher teaches everything right but the primary thing, he or she has nothing. Their message will keep them and their followers out of heaven and ultimately encourage people toward hell. This is extremely dangerous and very serious. What impact would it have if I continued to listen to their false gospel teaching over and over again, and quietly allow my friends, family members, and neighbors to do the same? What would the ultimate outcome be?

There are two possible options for dealing with a challenging situation like this: (1) attempts at reformation from inside the relationship with the false teacher, or (2) separation from the false teacher. Let's discuss these two options.

OPTION 1: REFORMATION FROM THE INSIDE

Because the consequences of a false gospel are so serious, there should *never* be an acceptance of error in this area. With this said, staying connected to a leader teaching a false gospel may be a *temporary* option as you wait to see if that teacher will reform his or her beliefs and teachings to align with the Bible.

As emotionally difficult as it can be, I believe every false gospel teacher and teaching should be confronted to protect others who could be led astray. It is never loving or right to leave cancer in place to spread and devastate the rest of the body. In the same way, it is never loving or right to notice a false gospel and remain silent about it, allowing more and more people to fall under its spiritually deadly grip. This may be a somewhat uncomfortable reality if this person is someone on television or a distant author, but it is especially difficult if it turns out this person is your father, mother, pastor, friend, spouse, professor, or mentor. Because the person is teaching a false gospel, that person is clearly not yet saved—even if they spend most of their time in the church. Without the true Gospel, they are lost and on their way toward judgment if they don't get on God's path to salvation. It is our responsibility to help the person see the truth and accept the salvation God offers—albeit with love, grace, and wise humility.

Earlier in my life, before I truly understood the Gospel as the Bible teaches it, I actively taught a false gospel while teaching Bible classes for the church I was attending. I thought I was going the right direction and wanted others to come along. I didn't know better and was teaching the same false gospel I had been taught by the major influencers in my life. I accepted these faulty explanations of the Bible's teachings and passed them on without really questioning if they were true. However, once I finally was confronted with a clear presentation of the Bible's description of the Gospel, I accepted it with open arms, and my teaching immediately changed to reflect this new biblical realization. This change of heart can happen after we confront a misguided teacher. If a change occurs, and a false teacher gets on the right track, it is the ideal outcome for a situation like this. Pray it occurs this way.

CONFRONTATION IS NECESSARY

As strange as it is, the apostle Paul even had to confront the apostle

Peter at one point. Peter was a wonderful man who had walked with Jesus, but he was only a *man*, subject to common human imperfections and weaknesses. For a while, Peter had been behaving as if a person had to obey the Law to be saved, and he was influencing others to act in similar ways. Out of love and concern for Peter and the others, Paul felt a responsibility to confront Peter regarding his error. Let's read this portion of Scripture to recall what took place:

> But when Peter came to Antioch, I had to oppose him to his face, for what he did was very wrong. When he first arrived, he ate with the Gentile believers, who were not circumcised. But afterward, when some friends of James came, Peter wouldn't eat with the Gentiles anymore. He was afraid of criticism from these people who insisted on the necessity of circumcision. As a result, other Jewish believers followed Peter's hypocrisy, and even Barnabas was led astray by their hypocrisy.

> When I saw that they were not following the truth of the gospel message, I said to Peter in front of all the others, "Since you, a Jew by birth, have discarded the Jewish laws and are living like a Gentile, why are you now trying to make these Gentiles follow the Jewish traditions?

> You and I are Jews by birth, not 'sinners' like the Gentiles. Yet we know that a person is made right with God by faith in Jesus Christ, not by obeying the law. And we have believed in Christ Jesus, so that we might be made right with God because of our faith in Christ, not because we have obeyed the law. For no one will ever be made right with God by obeying the law."

Galatians 2:11–16, NLT

The complexity of an influential leader teaching a false gospel is that others are likely to be led astray if this wrong teaching continues— led right out of true salvation and down a dangerous path that will lead people to an eternity in hell. This is no game to play around with.

Because Peter was negatively influencing others toward a wrong understanding of the Gospel, Paul stepped in to confront Peter. What was the result of this difficult but important confrontation? Peter later backed Paul firmly, saying:

> And count the patience of our Lord as salvation, just as our beloved brother Paul also wrote to you according to the wisdom given him, as he does in all his letters when he speaks in them of these matters.
>
> 2 Peter 3:15–16, ESV

Peter called Paul a "beloved brother" and noted Paul was a person who speaks with the wisdom and truth that comes from God. What a wonderful reconciliation! As time went on, God ultimately inspired Peter to write three books of the Bible, and each one is jam-packed with absolutely perfect Gospel teaching. With Paul and Peter, the results were exactly as one would hope: the confrontation of false teaching, humble acceptance of the rebuke and correction of that false teaching, and restoration to a biblical Gospel message—all with a good friendship still intact. This is reformation from *inside* a relationship, and in this case, the relationship could continue, perhaps stronger than ever. This is the ideal situation and one I believe God is always rooting for.

This approach should be preceded with fervent prayer, asking the Holy Spirit for an open door to speak, praying for the right words to say, and for a soft and receptive heart in the person you are approaching.

OPTION 2: SEPARATION

Unfortunately, some religious church leaders have never accepted the true Gospel message and have no intention of doing so. On the outside, they may look like any other believer, but on the inside, their view of the Gospel is skewed. They teach the Bible and talk about religious things, using their strong personalities to give their teachings an emotional boost, but they refuse the leading of God's Spirit toward the true path of salvation. Even after being confronted by the truth, they insist on continuing to teach a false gospel and spite the true Gospel message taught in the Bible. Some people refuse to believe God. Jesus said: "…You do not believe because you are not among my sheep. My sheep hear my voice, and I know them, and they follow me" (John 10:26–27, ESV). Some people decline Jesus' call to follow His voice as He tries to lead them toward the truth, and if this is the case with an influencer in your life, eventually you must leave this relationship, no matter how heartbreaking it is.

So how can leaving be done biblically? Jesus gave a helpful set of principles we may use in the sad case of having to deal with a person who continues to sin against others and God through teaching untruths. He said:

If another believer sins against you, go privately and point
out the offense. If the other person listens and confesses it,
you have won that person back. But if you are unsuccessful,
take one or two others with you and go back again, so that
everything you say may be confirmed by two or three
witnesses. If the person still refuses to listen, take your case
to the church. Then if he or she won't accept the church's
decision, treat that person as a pagan or a corrupt tax
collector.

Matthew 18:15_17, NLT

Willingly or unwillingly, to influence people toward a false gospel is
the greatest sin possible. It has the very real risk of leading people to
an eternally disastrous fate. Following the directions Jesus gave us,
we may follow these four steps when dealing with a false teacher
actively influencing others:

1. **PRIVATE MEETING.** Go privately to the person and point out the
   offense. Show what the Bible says about the true Gospel,
   and meet as long and as many times as it will take to give a
   full explanation and talk things out. Seek change and
   reconciliation.

2. **GROUP MEETING.** If the first approach is unsuccessful, take
   another person or two with you and approach the person in
   error once again. Perhaps the elders in your congregation
   would be a good option to bring into the conversation.
   Change and reconciliation are still the goals, but there will
   be multiple sources who recognize the problem if the person
   in error refuses to correct his or her teaching.

3. **PUBLIC CONFRONTATION.** If the person still refuses to change their
   ways and insists on continuing to teach a false gospel, then

you may communicate the issue to others in the church. A larger group may then confront the teacher in the setting of a corporate gathering. The goal is still a change of heart and reconciliation.

4. **SEPARATION.** Finally, if all three previous steps fail, and the false teacher continues to broadcast lies about the Gospel of Jesus, refusing to repent of this sinful unbelief, it is time to vacate the situation to prevent this negative influence from causing further harm. It is appropriate at this point to influence others to leave with you if they have also carefully followed the previous steps suggested by Jesus.

This is a difficult path Jesus prescribed, but He knew very well what was at stake. Eternity is on the line. If a forest fire insists on being a forest fire, we must run. You must separate yourself from a false teacher so that the lies and spiritual destruction do not spread. The Bible's teaching on the topic is clear:

> But even if we or an angel from heaven should preach to you a gospel contrary to the one we preached to you, let him be accursed. As we have said before, so now I say again: If anyone is preaching to you a gospel contrary to the one you received, let him be accursed.
> Galatians 1:8–9, ESV

It is no game to mess with the Gospel—God's one and only path to salvation.

If it is a friend or family member believing a false gospel but not actively influencing others to believe the same, you may want to give it time, continuing to pray and talk to that person as God leads you.

If a spouse is struggling with believing a false gospel, love them and patiently pray, share when it is appropriate, and be an example. False teaching is never an excuse to leave the lifelong commitment of marriage, so you must help them from within the marriage relationship. If you ever need to leave a situation through ceasing to watch a television show, getting rid of an author's books, or switching churches, you will need to ask God to lead you regarding how to do this (i.e., timing, attitude, next steps, etc.). Remember, you are a believer and a representative of Jesus, so whatever you do must be done with love, lots of prayer, and full reliance on God's wisdom. Such a move should never be done out of bitterness or being led by intense emotions; it should be done with careful thought and sorrow in your heart over the choices the false teacher is making. Ultimately it is not your fault for any necessary separation that takes place; instead, it is due to the continued sinful choices of the false gospel teacher.

UNITY IS GOD'S WILL

Church unity is God's will and His *Plan A*. Whenever possible; we should seek peace and solidarity in the church, family, and community. Yet under the most extreme circumstances—such as when someone is actively teaching a false gospel—there is a time and place for separation. Again, the souls of your family, friends, and neighbors are at stake, so do not remain passive and silent.

Part 6

CAN A BELIEVER LOSE SALVATION?

Chapter 23

HIT BY A MALFUNCTIONING PLANE WHILE LOOKING AT PORN IN A SECOND-STORY APARTMENT

WHEN IT COMES to the devil's strategy with *unbelievers,* he desperately wants the entire sin concept to be out of sight and out of mind. He desires this ignorance because he is dreadfully afraid that if people recognize their sin and guilt, they may recognize they need a Savior. He knows any thought of a Savior would be a great defeat to his malevolent battle plan, so *sin* is a topic Satan tries to avoid.

However, for dealing with *believers* in Jesus, the devil must use a completely different tactic. With believers, the devil's goal must be to destroy their faith in Jesus and get them to stop believing He is sufficient to save them. To do this, the devil must get the believer to fall into self-righteousness, believing strict obedience to God's law will earn them heaven (which implicitly accepts the lie that Jesus is not adequate). If the devil's trap of prideful self-righteousness doesn't work, he tries the other side of the same coin: *condemnation.* With this tactic, the devil tries to get a believer to fixate on his or her failures and feel unworthy of being saved by Jesus. The devil loves to shine his spotlight on the believer's sin, and yell out: "Look at you, dirty wretch. You believe that Man will save you? Not quite. There is no so-called 'amazing grace' for something as ugly as you. Such pigs cannot pray; they cannot hope to have a relationship with God. Heaven has no place for a sinner like you. You're lost." Through this vicious onslaught, the devil attempts to kill a believer's peace and assurance of salvation by confusing the person into thinking he or she is too dirty for God.

Condemnation is the devil's profession—it's what he does best. He does not relent, and he attacks again and again with absolutely no disposition toward mercy. It is no wonder the Bible refers to him as "the accuser of our brethren" (Revelation 12:10, NKJV) and reports he "prowls around like a roaring lion looking for someone to devour" (1 Peter 5:8, NIV). Have you ever experienced these attacks? If you have then you are like every other member of God's family, each one living with a target on his or her back, all having to stand our ground in the faith against the devil's fiery darts of accusation. We must stand strong.

OBSERVING THE ENEMY

To help us prepare for these attacks on our faith, it's good to become acquainted with the enemy's methods of attack. Here are a handful of examples of how the devil's accusation may hit us:

- "Hey, I just want to inform you that your sin is far too extensive for God to accept you."
- "For your information, no *real* believer would sin like you have this week."

- "Look—you did it again! What a failure! You've stumbled over the same sin too many times now. You'll never make it into heaven."
- "Tonight was a disaster. Obviously, you haven't turned away from your sins enough to be worthy of God's forgiveness."
- "You have blasphemed the Holy Spirit with your sin. You've committed the unforgivable sin. Salvation is out of reach for you now."
- "Why even try? You know you're no good at this 'religion' thing. Now is the perfect time to give up."
- "Everyone in your faith community knows about your horrible sin. They're all looking down on you. You don't fit there."

Welcome to war—the war against your soul. These statements and many others like them are the flaming arrows that the devil shoots toward the hearts of believers in Jesus. We need to have our shields up.

PORN, AN AIRPLANE, AND A SECOND-STORY WINDOW

So how should we think about a believer in Jesus who sins, and what if that person even ends up dying while in the act of sinning? Will he go to hell? Let's consider an illustration to help us answer these questions and surface an important Gospel principle. Imagine there was a man who lived in the second story of an apartment building located right next to a busy airport. This fellow had accepted Jesus as his Savior a few years earlier. He held on to this faith in Jesus day-by-day, retaining a constant trust that the sin-cleansing work Jesus accomplished on the cross was fully enough to save him from his sins and make him right with God.

One day the man came home after a long day at the office. He climbed the stairs to his apartment, entered his bedroom, flipped open his laptop computer, and against everything he knew to be right, looked at pornography. While this man was still in the middle of the act, willfully viewing the graphic images and deliberately committing this sin against God, a malfunctioning aircraft from the airport next door happened to veer off the runway and crash directly into the second-story room where the porn-viewing was taking place. The man at the laptop was killed instantly. He didn't even know what hit him. Here is the question: Would this man go to heaven or hell?

FOCUSING ON THE RIGHT THING

When attempting to answer this question about the porn incident, maybe our initial instinct is to focus on the deviant behavior of the believer. Some might look at his actions and deliver the following judgment: "He was looking at porn when he died. Yes, he was a believer, but his life ended while he was willfully choosing to sin. He knew better. Furthermore, he didn't even have time to repent or ask for forgiveness. The guy would go straight to hell for his behavior." This behavior-oriented answer fixates on the wrong thing by focusing on the sin and ignoring the faith. If you look back at our illustration, you'll notice the following was said about the man before he died:

> "... [T]his fellow had accepted Jesus as his Savior a few years earlier. He held on to this faith day by day, retaining a constant trust that the sin-cleansing work Jesus accomplished on the cross was enough to save him from his sins and make him right with God."

When determining whether a person is saved, a true believer in Jesus, and a citizen of heaven or hell, the correct question to ask is: "Does the person in question trust Jesus as his personal Savior?" If the answer to the previous question is "yes," then there is no condemnation for that person—even if he died while sinning. The man was a sinner before he was saved, and after believing in Jesus, he was forgiven and made right with God. Why would we think the conditions for salvation changed *after* he became a believer?

The presence or absence of *faith* is the correct place to focus on when determining whether a person is saved. The presence or absence of good *behavior* is not the right area to focus on because everyone's behavior falls short of God's standard. (See Romans 3:23 and James 2:10) The faith-filled person has had his past and present sins washed away, and God considers that person to be as legally sinless as Jesus. Is this sin-cleansing work of Jesus really enough to save this believer from hell even if this person died in the midst of the foolish sin of looking at pornography? Absolutely.

THE FRUSTRATION OF THE SELF-RIGHTEOUS

Some readers will likely feel unsettled at this point. In fact, both the devil and self-righteous persons find the freedom of this biblical, Jesus-centered Gospel to be repulsive and infuriating. The devil hates it because he knows this true Gospel message has the power to save the guilty human soul from the condemnation it deserves. The cross event is the very real, victorious defense that believers can appeal to while standing against the devil's brutal accusations.

The self-righteous person also hates this message. The gift of salvation through faith in Jesus takes all the glory away from the self-righteous man's efforts, pulling the rug out from under his pride. If salvation is a gift, then there isn't any rational ground for boasting. Yet the self-righteous are proud of their good behavior, and gain comfort from believing they are better than their neighbors. They say, "God forbid that a person who sins often could be saved and enter the kingdom of heaven." These people forget they too are considered dirty, untouchable sinners in the eyes of a holy God if they are without the guilt-removing work of Jesus.

Both the devil and the self-righteous "religious" folk often work for the same team, zealously urging people to focus their attention away from the Savior and onto themselves and their own efforts. Beware.

JESUS PAID IT ALL

I was once a self-righteous young man, convinced my right standing with God could be bought by my strong moral performance. I would argue against grace:

> "There is no way a person can be saved by simply believing and saying a prayer. If obtaining and maintaining salvation were really that easy, what would stop people from sinning? There would be no threat of hell, so there would be no motivation to obey. The teaching that a person is saved only by having faith in Jesus as Savior would give the person a 'license to sin.'"

This, of course, flaunted my misunderstanding of the Gospel. What most people on the outside didn't realize was I had such a difficult time ever feeling assured of my salvation. I drastically fluctuated between my days of good behavior in which I felt saved and my bad days in which I felt unsaved. It all depended on my performance.

The truth was the more carefully and honestly I analyzed my self-righteous life, the more sin I saw in myself.

I was better than 99 percent of the people who were out there. I guarded my actions and thoughts against sin almost as well as was humanly possible. But there was a problem: Even though many people around me thought I was a solid role model of godliness, I knew in my heart that even the most microscopic sins were heavy enough in God's holy eyes to drag me all the way to the pit of hell. God was far, far more holy than my self-righteous heart ever imagined. The more I got to know God and His standard, the more I realized I was utterly failing to live up to that standard. God's standard is no less than *perfection*—a brutal, unrelenting, inexorable standard for the self-righteous man. So God had to bring me to the breaking point where I finally realized my goodness could never earn right standing with Him. Jesus paid for it all without my help. I had to learn to trust completely and exclusively in His finished work on the cross if I wanted to be saved from the condemnation I deserved.

Now, what about you? Do you fully trust Jesus to save you from your sins? If so, then you don't have to fear a thing from the Accuser or his self-righteous emissaries. You have a Savior who is perfectly able to hold you in the safety of His salvation—even when the devil parades all your weaknesses in a mile-long procession before your eyes. Jesus can save you even if you die while looking at pornography or committing some other sin. I encourage you to do your best to live an obedient life before God because of all the unmerited kindness He has shown you, but please also hold firm to your faith in Jesus when you fail. He will not fail you.

But when Christ had offered for all time a single sacrifice
for sins, he sat down at the right hand of God...
Hebrews 10:12, ESV

— *Chapter 24* —

THE SILVER WIRE OF FAITH

My dear children, I am writing this to you so that you will not sin.
But if anyone does sin, we have an advocate who pleads our case before
the Father. He is Jesus Christ, the one who is truly righteous.
1 John 2:1, NLT

SOME PEOPLE HOLD the view that once someone attains salvation through faith in Jesus as Savior, they must then maintain it by a lifestyle of good behavior to keep it. Their mantra goes a bit like this: "First *attain* salvation, then *maintain* to *retain*." These people think if a believer falls into some sinful behavior, she is at high risk of losing her salvation by being tossed right out of God's family. In their view, if a believer's sin crosses a certain point, it will change that person's eternal destination from heaven to hell solely based on their bad performance.

Because every believer in the world sins in some manner every day, this perspective can be a very distressing point of view for people who take an honest look at their lives and compare it to God's holiness. So how exactly *does* God deal with the believer in Jesus who sins?

THE SILVER WIRE

Envision a man who is hearing a presentation of the good news of Jesus for the first time. As he intently listens, God drops a shiny, silver wire down from heaven to where the man is standing. The glistening wire dangles in front of his face. Immediately, at the very moment faith appears within his heart, that tiny, silver wire hanging from heaven attaches itself firmly to the heart of this new believer.

In this story, the silver wire is a visual representation of the faith that exists in someone who has trusted in Jesus as his Savior. The moment the unbeliever believes, trusting that Jesus died on the cross to save him from the penalty of sin and make him right with God, he establishes his connection to God. He is forgiven and saved by faith. As long as this man continues to possess this same saving faith within his heart, he will continue to be connected to God, in right standing with Him. As long as the silver wire of faith is connected, God considers the substitutionary punishment that Jesus received on the cross to be sufficient payment for this man's sins. The man stands guilt-free before God in a *legal* sense. He is legally holy.

THE SILVER WIRE REMAINS

Yet the question remains: How exactly does God deal with the believer in Jesus who commits sins? Jumping back into our story, fast forward as this new believer lives out his life of faith. Day and night, everywhere he goes, that shiny, silver wire of faith continues to connect him to God and the forgiveness that comes through Jesus. Moment by moment, everywhere he goes he is in a constant state of faith; he believes Jesus is the Savior God sent to rescue him from his sin guilt and to make him right with God. On through life, he goes. Monday through Friday he heads off to work. He attends gatherings with his community of faith on the weekends. He plays soccer with his friends at the park once in a while. He surfs the internet in the evening after work, and he periodically sneaks a peek at an objectionable website. He cooks dinner in the evenings. He gets up ten minutes early for work on Tuesday morning so that he can make time to pray. He slips up and tells a lie to his co-worker.

He gets married. He contributes money to a new homeless shelter. He cheats a little bit on his taxes. He watches TV. He goes on a mission and aid trip to Haiti with a group of believers. He gets jealous of his neighbor's new car. He donates money to a charity for underprivileged children, and on and on life goes for this man.

As we can see, our fellow lives a life made up of both good and bad thoughts and activities. He is a believer, and yet he still sins. He carries with him that silver wire of faith everywhere he goes. Yes, whether this man is engaged in good or evil, his faith in Jesus attaches him to the heart of God and assures him of continual forgiveness for any sin he may commit. Amazingly, even during those careless moments when he is directly committing a sin, his silver wire of faith is never broken. He continues to believe Jesus is his Savior, and trusts in Jesus alone to save him from his sin guilt. Some days are better than others. This continual faith in Jesus' finished work on the cross perpetually saves the believer and keeps him connected to God—even on the bad days.

FAITH IN JESUS: PERPETUAL SALVATION FOR A BELIEVER WHO SINS

It always saddens God when we sin, and sin often brings about trouble in our lives. Like any familial relationship, sin can cause feelings of relational strain between us and our Heavenly Father. Yet salvation has and always will be a gift from God—free for us, yet purchased with the priceless blood of Jesus as He hung on the cross, bearing the guilt and punishment for our sins upon His shoulders. It is through our moment-by-moment faith in Jesus that we continue to be saved from old and new sins alike. So if you are a believer, you will feel (and should feel) significant sorrow in your heart when you disobey your Heavenly Father. This sorrow is healthy, and it urges you to think twice before you make the same mistake again. However, if you are a believer, you should always be at peace deep within your soul. Like the man in our story, you initially attain your salvation through *faith in Jesus*, and you maintain and retain your salvation through continuing on in that same *faith in Jesus*.

— Chapter 25 —

THE ONE AND ONLY ONE WAY TO LOSE YOUR SALVATION

NTERESTINGLY ENOUGH, the Scriptures make it clear there *is* one way for salvation to be lost. Long ago, the Apostle Paul wrote a letter to the churches and synagogues that were located in the ancient region of Galatia—a letter we have already discussed. In this letter, he firmly scolded the Galatian believers for moving away from the pure saving faith they had once held. After having trusted in Jesus alone for their salvation, these people had foolishly allowed false teachers to influence their congregations. These false teachers taught salvation needed to be obtained through faith in Jesus *and* also through obedience to the Old Testament commandments. These deceivers were pushing a perspective upon Galatian believers that caused them to fear faith in Jesus was not enough to save them. Out of intense love and concern, Paul sternly chastised the Galatians:

> I am astonished that you are so quickly deserting the one who called you to live in the grace of Christ and are turning to a different gospel—which is really no gospel at all. Evidently some people are throwing you into confusion and are trying to pervert the gospel of Christ.
> Galatians 1:6–7, NIV

His corrective rebuke continued:

> I do not treat the grace of God as meaningless. For if keeping the law could make us right with God, then there was no need for Christ to die. Oh, foolish Galatians! Who has cast an evil spell on you? For the meaning of Jesus Christ's death was made as clear to you as if you had seen a picture of his death on the cross. Let me ask you this one question: Did you receive the Holy Spirit by obeying the law of Moses? Of course not! You received the Spirit because you believed the message you heard about Christ.
> Galatians 2:21–3:2, NLT

Here we find a biblical example of a group of believers who had once been soundly saved through trusting in Jesus' sin-cleansing work on the cross, yet these children of God were deceived into believing they needed more than Jesus to obtain salvation. Being convinced by the false teachers that they needed to diligently obey God's law if they wanted to be saved by Jesus, they accepted a false Gospel that suggested a man is saved by one part Jesus and one part good behavior. Without even knowing it, they converted away from the true religion of the Bible to a perverted, diluted version that had no real power to save. Paul finishes with a strong exhortation and a scorching warning:

> So Christ has truly set us free. Now make sure that you stay free, and don't get tied up again in slavery to the law. Listen! I, Paul, tell you this: If you are counting on [obedience to the biblical laws] to make you right with God, then Christ will be of no benefit to you. I'll say it again. If you are trying to find favor with God by [obeying the laws of God], you must obey every regulation in the whole law of Moses. For if you are trying to make yourselves right with God by keeping

the law, you have been cut off from Christ! You have fallen away from God's grace.
Galatians 5:1–4, NLT

Could Paul be any clearer? He expressed the crushing consequences of the people's decision to trust in their works to help them earn salvation as a supplement to their faith in the Savior. Paul declared this decision put them in a state where they had "fallen away from God's grace" and become "estranged from Christ."

We conclude there is only one thing that can cause a believer to lose his salvation and to "fall from God's grace": A believer can and *will* forfeit salvation if he stops believing Jesus' sacrificial death is the exclusive means for salvation. Salvation is lost if a believer stops believing or adds another condition to Jesus' substitutionary death. In either case, this person has become an *unbeliever*. Saving faith must always remain established, and saving faith must always remain exclusive. To redirect our faith in any way other than exclusive trust in Jesus to save us is to cut that silver wire of faith that connects us with God. If we don't have the faith required by God to apply for forgiveness that Jesus won for us when He bore the punishment we deserve, how can we hope to escape punishment for our sins?

THE BACKUP PARACHUTE OF WORKS

Imagine a person was to go skydiving. The plane takes off, rises 13,000 feet above the ground, the jump door opens, and the jumper stands at the edge, looking at the clouds a mile or two down and the land even further below. The jumper has secured her parachute on her back, but as she weighs the potential consequences of her jump, she turns and looks back behind her at the seat where the smaller backup parachute lies. "Should I put it on?" she wonders.

The jumper in this illustration is having a dilemma of faith. If she truly had 100 percent faith that her primary parachute would save her, she would never consider going through the trouble of putting on a backup parachute, would she? However, if there were the slightest doubt in her mind the primary parachute would fail her, she would add a backup chute—just in case. All it would take is 99 percent faith in the primary parachute yet 1 percent doubt, and she would resist putting full reliance on the primary chute. It takes full faith in a parachute to jump without a backup. The very presence of a backup implies the jumper does not have *true* faith in the primary chute.

If planes and parachutes had existed back in Paul's day, he might have used the parachute illustration in his critique of the Galatians, saying:

> "You who are jumping from the plane of life must put your full, exclusive faith in the one and only saving Parachute God has ever provided for you: *Jesus.* You Galatians should trust His sacrificial work will certainly save you from all your sins, making you perfectly blameless before God and ready to confidently face Him on judgment day. Yet I am saddened to see someone has come along and tricked you into believing Jesus is not enough to save you. Now I see you are wearing the Backup Parachute of Morality, trusting your good and moral behavior will somehow play a part in saving you. Foolish Galatians! Why are you wearing that worthless reserve? Isn't Jesus' work enough to save you? Your backup parachute is proof you no longer fully trust in Jesus, the Primary Parachute."

STAND FIRM IN THE FAITH

There is no need to fear losing salvation if you firmly believe. Continue in your faith in Jesus (Jesus + Nothing = Salvation). Let us all stand strong in this faith with perseverance, trusting that Jesus' sacrifice alone paid the full price to relieve us of the guilt and punishment we deserved for our sins. If we ever realize we are walking down the same perilous path the Galatians were warned about, allowing our faith to become diluted and nullified by trusting in something other than Jesus alone, then we must straighten our path and reaffirm our faith. We must reconnect our disconnected silver wire of faith.

The Gospel forever will be only about Jesus, and His final words while hanging on the cross were: "It is finished!" Let us trust His words to the end, believing our salvation was paid for in full two thousand years ago on a cross in the city of Jerusalem.

*Once you were alienated from God and were enemies
in your minds because of your evil behavior. But now He has
reconciled you by Christ's physical body through death to present
you holy in His sight, without blemish and free from accusation
—if you continue in your faith, established and firm, and do not
move from the hope held out in the Gospel. This is the Gospel
that you heard and that has been proclaimed to every creature
under heaven, and of which I, Paul, have become a servant.*
Colossians 1:21–23, NIV

— *Chapter 26* —

DO ALL SMOKERS GO TO HELL?

S OMETIMES I HEAR people say to get into heaven you must "believe in Jesus and turn away from your sins." Others are willing to overlook "mistakes," but they say any believer engaged in "habitual sin" is certainly not going to make it to heaven. Is it really true that people must turn away from their sins to be rescued by Jesus? Good question.

SMOKING OUR WAY TO HELL?

It is a scientific fact that smoking significantly harms a smoker's lungs, and willfully harming our bodies is a sin, no doubt. First Corinthians 6:19–20 teaches us: "Do you not know that your bodies are temples of the Holy Spirit, who is in you, whom you have received from God? You are not your own; you were bought at a price. Therefore honor God with your bodies" (NIV). Harming the body through a cigarette addiction is a daily, repetitive sin. Now here's my question: If turning away from your sin was a precondition for salvation, what would happen to believers who struggle with smoking addictions? Are all those habitually sinning smokers in our churches driving in the fast lane on the highway to hell?

While I think smoking is repulsive, all you smokers who have trusted in Jesus as your Savior can relax and take a deep breath (if you are able). You are not going to be thrown into hell for this habitual sin. Because of your faith in Jesus, you are on your way to heaven—although you may get there sooner than non-smokers.

DON'T THINK THAT SMOKING IS A SIN? WHAT ABOUT THE SABBATH?

If you haven't been convinced smoking is really a sin, then let's talk about the Ten Commandments. The Ten Commandments include important laws for society including the commands not to lie, cheat with another person's spouse, steal, worship idols, and so forth. One common, weekly, and habitual sin is the breaking of the Sabbath Law—also one of the Ten Commandments. The Bible says: "Remember the Sabbath day, to keep it holy" (Exodus 20:8, NKJV). This law is helpful for our emotional health and for our ability to smile and love others. Those who refuse to follow God's commandment to take a day off each week rob themselves, others, and God of the heart devotion they deserve. It would be a difficult thing to disregard the authority of any one of the Ten Commandments, and the same question must be brought up for those who habitually break the Sabbath commandment: Do all believers who repetitively, habitually, and unrepentantly break the Sabbath get thrown into hell for their Sabbath-breaking?

BACK TO REALITY

The truth is all believers continue to sin to some extent, even after they come to faith. The first category of sin is called the *Sins of Commission*, and this refers to the things we shouldn't have done but did anyway. This is the category most people think about when sin is brought up.

The second category is called the *Sins of Omission*, and these are the things we should have done but didn't do. This second realm of sin is often much more subtle than the first, and human beings are notoriously lazy in their self-critique about the sins of omission. Because of this, these sins often go overlooked. The result is humans commonly think more highly of themselves than they should.

Everyone is guilty of making sin a habit in our lives in one way or another. Here is a little evidence that should prove this point well. The following is a long (but greatly incomplete) list of sins we all frequently stumble upon, and it includes bad things we do and good things we fail to do. Here are several lists:

INTERNAL SINS OF THE HEART

Pride, envy, lust, impatience, judgmental attitude, selfishness, bitterness, unforgiveness, greed, unrighteous anger, not genuinely rejoicing when the success of others exceeds your own, doing good things to be seen by other people rather than by God, hypocrisy, selfish ambition, self-righteous thinking, ungratefulness, etc.

EXTERNAL SINS

Speaking white lies or deceptive incomplete truths, arguing, misrepresenting numbers at tax time, gossiping, listening to gossip, complaining, not respecting authority, laziness, not submitting to the laws of the land (such as speed limits), stealing little things (such as paper clips from work), breaking God's commandment of taking a Sabbath rest, etc.

SINS OF OMISSION

Not giving generously to the poor, not being kind, not spending time with the emotionally needy, not visiting the sick, not proactively helping those in need, not fulfilling the Great Commission by sharing the truth when we could have, not honoring our father and mother like we should have, not honoring our grandparents like we should have, not loving our spouse like we should have, not being merciful, not constantly loving all others as we love ourselves, not loving God with all our heart, etc.

SINS IN OUR RELATIONSHIP WITH GOD

Not trusting God's promises, putting a busy schedule before our relationship with God, fearing what people think more than what God thinks (and acting as such), worshipping God with our words but without an engaged heart during a worship service, not cherishing God's Bible as we should, etc.

Do you struggle with any of these sins? Let me answer this simple question for you: Yes, you do. We all do on a recurring basis. You are a habitual sinner.

JESUS SOLVED THE PROBLEM

What person will really come out and say, "You must turn from your sin to be saved"? Any person who teaches this impossible prerequisite is proclaiming condemnation on his head. Salvation is not earned by the two-fold prescription of (1) turning from sin and (2) trusting in Jesus. Instead, salvation will always be a gift given to unworthy sinners who trust in Jesus alone to save them from their sin guilt from start to finish. We are habitual sinners, but thank God Jesus is a habitual Forgiver!

But now apart from the law the righteousness has been made
known, to which the Law and the Prophets testify. This righteousness
is given through faith in Jesus Christ to all who believe.
Romans 3:21–22, NIV

Part 7

THE THREE THINGS EVERYONE SHOULD KNOW

Chapter 27

UNDERSTANDING JUDGMENT DAY 101

MANY PEOPLE WONDER if sin really matters. After all, we've all sinned thousands of times throughout our lives, and God has never really visibly held us accountable. So when it comes down to it, many people wonder, "Why does sin matter at all?" There *will* come a day when sin guilt will become dreadfully important—a day when accounts are settled between God and sinners—a day of *judgment*. In the following, we will explore all the Bible has to teach about this imminent day called "Judgment Day."

WHAT IS "SIN"?

Sin is any thought or action that goes against the will of God. Sins might be the things we think, the bad things we do, and/or the good things we fail to do.

WILL HUMAN BEINGS BE JUDGED FOR THEIR SINS?

Yes, every human being will one day stand before the judgment seat of God. The Bible says: "…Each person is destined to die once and after that comes judgment…" (Hebrews 9:27, NLT). (See also John 5:24–29, 2 Peter 2:4–9, and Revelation 20:11–15)

WHO WILL JUDGE HUMAN BEINGS?

Jesus of Nazareth, Israel will be the judge of human beings on judgment day. We read the words of Jesus: "The Father judges no one, but has entrusted all judgment to the Son, that all may honor the Son just as they honor the Father. Whoever does not honor the Son does not honor the Father, who sent Him" (John 5:22–23, NIV). (See also Romans 2:16, 2 Timothy 4:1, and John 5:26–27)

WHEN ARE A PERSON'S FATES SEALED?

Once a person dies there is no changing their fate. There is no reincarnation, no purgatory, and no second chances of any kind. Each person will die as either a *forgiven believer* or as an *unforgiven unbeliever*. While everyone will ultimately see Jesus when they die, and everyone will believe when they see Him, if a person dies as an unforgiven unbeliever they will remain unforgiven for eternity. Again, a person's fate is unalterably sealed upon death.

WILL SOME PEOPLE BE JUDGED AS "GUILTY"?

Yes. The final judgment day will certainly take place, and every unbeliever will be held accountable and be judged "guilty" for their sins. Every unbeliever's sins are recorded for use in this heavenly court for accurately judging, convicting, and sentencing the sinner.

Because the unbeliever did not put their trust in the Savior God sent, their names will not be found in Jesus' Book of Life and will condemned for their sin and thrown into a place of eternal judgment called the lake of fire (See Revelation 20:11–15, John 3:18, John 3:36, and John 5:25–29).

WILL SOME MAKE IT THROUGH JUDGMENT DAY WITHOUT BEING CONDEMNED?

Yes—some people will make it through God's judgment without being condemned, and this is the good news of the Gospel. Those who have accepted Jesus as their Savior will not face the judgment in the same way unbelievers will. All people have sinned and incurred guilt, however, those who believe in Jesus have already had their sin guilt dealt with through Jesus' death. Out of love, Jesus took all the punishment for their sins upon Himself so that they don't have to be punished.

Those who have trusted in Jesus as their Savior will be *acquitted* of all charges and there will not be any condemnation or punishment. Those believers have their names listed in Jesus' Book of Life because they believed in Him, and they will be welcomed into heaven, which is their heavenly Father's home. (See Revelation 20:11–15, Revelation 21–22, John 3:18, Romans 5:9, 2 Corinthians 5:21, Hebrews 9:26–28, and Hebrews 10:10)

WHAT IS THE MOST DETAILED VERSE IN THE BIBLE FOR DESCRIBING JUDGMENT DAY?

One Bible passage provides a particularly in-depth description of the judgment day we all must face. John, a disciple of Jesus and one of His closest friends, was given a vision by Jesus and told to write it down. Here is what it says:

> Then I saw a great white throne and him who was seated on it. The earth and the heavens fled from his presence, and there was no place for them. And I saw the dead, great and small, standing before the throne, and books were opened. Another book was opened, which is the book of life. The dead were judged according to what they had done as recorded in the books. The sea gave up the dead that were in it, and death and Hades gave up the dead that were in them, and each person was judged according to what they had done. Then death and Hades were thrown into the lake of fire. The lake of fire is the second death. Anyone whose name was not found written in the book of life was thrown into the lake of fire.
>
> Revelation 20:11–15, NIV

Notice that "books were opened," and there was another book opened, which is the "Book of Life." The first books have the records of every sin ever committed by the unforgiven sinners being judged. The second book—the Book of Life—has the names of all who have trusted in Jesus and had their slates wiped perfectly clean and are forgiven, freed from all judgment for their sins, fully reconciled to God, and will have an eternal home in heaven.

Chapter 28

UNDERSTANDING HELL 101

THE BIBLE TEACHES about two places *unbelievers* go after they die, one being a temporary place known as "hell" and another being an eternal place known as "the Lake of Fire." This setup is similar to modern legal and penal systems. Today, we have two places: *Jail* and *Prison*. Jails hold individuals as they await their trial, and prison is the long-term place of punishment for criminals after the trial and sentencing have occurred. Hell and the lake of fire work in a similar way: hell is like the temporary jail, and the lake of fire is like the long-term prison.

WHAT IS "HELL"?

Unbelieving human beings will officially be judged and condemned for their sins on judgment day. Before this, unbelievers die and leave their bodies in the grave, and their spirits leave their bodies to go to a place the Bible calls hell (also known as "hades" in the Greek language of the New Testament[6]). Hades is a short-term waiting place where unbelievers must stay before their judgment day trial. (See Revelation 20:11–15 for more details) It is important to note

---

[6] "G86 - hadēs – Strong's Greek Lexicon (KJV)." Blue Letter Bible. https://www.blueletterbible.org//lang/lexicon/lexicon.cfm?Strongs=G86&t=KJV

the Bible's original language makes clear distinctions between the names and the purposes of the short-term place of holding called hell and the long-term place of punishment called the lake of fire.

WHAT IS THE "LAKE OF FIRE"?

The Bible teaches the lake of fire is the final place of punishment for unbelievers who have not received forgiveness through faith in Jesus. When judgment day arrives, all unbelievers will be transferred from hell (where they were awaiting their trial and sentencing) to the White Throne judgment seat of Christ. There they will be judged according to their thoughts and actions. Unbelievers will be found "guilty" for transgressing God's law and their unbelief in Jesus, God's chosen Savior (See John 3:18). These unbelievers will be justly condemned for their sin-crimes against God, and they will be eternally sentenced to a place of punishment the Bible calls the lake of fire ("Gehenna" in the original Greek language). (See Revelation 20:10–15, Revelation 21:8, Revelation 19:20, Matthew 13:49–50, Matthew 25:41, 2 Thessalonians 1:9)

WHO WILL BE IN THE LAKE OF FIRE?

Satan, his demons (fallen angels), and every unbelieving human whose name is not found in Jesus' Book of Life will one day be thrown into the lake of fire. (See Matthew 25:41, Revelation 20:10, and Revelation 20:11–15)

WHY WILL PEOPLE BE PUNISHED IN THE LAKE OF FIRE?

Unbelievers will be justly punished because they have sinned against the Holy God and have rejected Jesus the Savior. All human beings ultimately incur guilt and condemn themselves by the sins they commit. God knew every individual is self-condemned by their evil choices, so out of His great love for humanity, He designed a plan through which a sinner could be freed from the guilt of sin. God's solution was Jesus.

Jesus' sacrificial work on the cross has the potential to bring forgiveness, acquittal from sin guilt, and a full reconciliation to God for all who will accept Jesus by faith. However, God will force no one to accept this free offer of salvation. If a person rejects the Savior's gift and the forgiveness He offers, God honors the gift of choice He gave to everyone. (See Matthew 13:41-42, John 3:18, John 3:36, and Romans 6:23)

Chapter 29

UNDERSTANDING HEAVEN 101

THE BIBLE DESCRIBES a wonderful place where *believers* go after they die, and believers often call this place "Heaven." This is one of the great promises of the faith! There are some interesting nuances to the biblical teachings on this exciting destination. As we survey some of what the Bible has to say about the future of believers, one might say there are *two* different heavens—but not exactly. Let's take a look to make sense of things.

WHAT IS "HEAVEN/PARADISE"?

Heaven is the place Jesus referred to as "Paradise" while He was being crucified. Jesus looked to His side and told the criminal hanging beside Him that he would be with Jesus in "Paradise" that very day (Luke 23:42–43). Why was this criminal and sinner counted worthy of this ultimate blessing? The reason is the criminal believed in Jesus while they were both hanging there together. The criminal's faith in Jesus saved him.

Heaven ("Paradise") is the place where God the Father and Jesus dwell now, along with the spirits of all believers who have ever died since the creation of the world. (See 2 Corinthians 5:8, Philippians 1:22–24, and Romans 8:34) This is the place where the souls of believers wait until the resurrection of all dead believers at Jesus' second coming. (See 1 Thessalonians 4:16–17 and 1 Corinthians 15:50–58) God knows those who have believed in the sin-atoning sacrifice of Jesus and those who did not, and upon death each human is assigned his or her place accordingly.

WHAT IS THE "NEW JERUSALEM"?

The "New Jerusalem" is the name God gave the dwelling place prepared as the ultimate, final, eternal home for the believers of all ages. This eternal home will be the inheritance of every believer directly following the final judgment. The New Jerusalem is where believers will live with God forever (See Revelation 21–22). This is likely the place Jesus was referring to when He said, "Do not let your hearts be troubled. You believe in God; believe also in me. My Father's house has many rooms; if that were not so, would I have told you that I am going there to prepare a place for you? And if I go and prepare a place for you, I will come back and take you to be with me that you also may be where I am" (John 14:1–3, NIV). For a detailed description of the "Father's house," which is the New Jerusalem, read the 21st and 22nd chapters of the book of Revelation.

WHAT WILL IT BE LIKE IN THE NEW JERUSALEM?

This current world will not last forever, and the Bible clearly teaches this (See 2 Peter 3:9–13 and Revelation 21:1). At the end of the world, this will be the beginning of never-ending happiness for believers as they move on to live with the God they love as He reveals more and more of His goodness to His people (Again, see Revelation 21–22). Describing this future home, the Apostle John tells us:

> Then I saw a new heaven and a new earth, for the first heaven and the first earth had passed away, and the sea was no more. And I saw the holy city, new Jerusalem, coming down out of heaven from God, prepared as a bride adorned for her husband. And I heard a loud voice from the throne saying, "Behold, the dwelling place of God is with man. He will dwell with them, and they will be his people, and God himself will be with them as their God. He will wipe away every tear from their eyes, and death shall be no more, neither shall there be mourning, nor crying, nor pain anymore, for the former things have passed away."
> Revelation 21:1–4, ESV

WHO WILL BE IN THE NEW JERUSALEM?

Believers will be counted "not guilty" on Judgment Day because they have trusted in and received the atonement for sin paid for through Jesus' work on the cross. Through this, they will gain access to the New Jerusalem after the Judgment Day. It is true that every human being that has ever lived has sinned and fallen far short of God's glorious standard of perfection. These people will be spared all judgment and will find their eternal citizenship to be in the New Jerusalem with their God and Savior. All because of Jesus!

Part 8

CONCLUSION:
THE GAME PLAN

Chapter 30

THE CHURCH: THE GREATEST MISSION FIELD IN THE WORLD

W E HAVE ARRIVED at the end of this book. The victorious cross event is the very linchpin of our faith, and without it, everything falls apart, and religion becomes meaningless. Without the cross, we miss God's main point. With this said, above all we must preserve this Gospel message, protecting its integrity, teaching it faithfully to others, and continuously reminding ourselves of this good news. This has been the purpose of this book.

PREACHING THE GOSPEL TO UNBELIEVERS IN CHURCH

As the early church was not immune to false Gospel representations, so it remains today. I hope by now we have all recognized there are three distinct groups of people in our churches today, including:

1. **BELIEVERS:** People who have accepted the Gospel and are saved.
2. **UNBELIEVERS:** People who haven't chosen to accept the Gospel and are not saved.

3. **STILL UNBELIEVERS:** People who have accepted a false Gospel—and are not saved.

Why does awareness of this third category above matter so much? Because the church remains the single greatest mission field in the world! Millions of people sit in pews each Sunday with hearts wide open to God, and yet even with all the religious flurrying around them, a significant number remain unconverted in their souls. Many have not been taught the biblical truth a sinner must rely on the Savior alone to be saved. I know this to be true because I was once one of these people—fully "religious," yet wholly unaware of what the true Gospel teaches. No wonder I felt so miserable! Religiosity without assurance of salvation is a miserable state of existence. Readers who now understand "Jesus plus nothing equals salvation" ought to recognize Jesus' call to go into all the world to preach His Gospel—even if that means helping friends at our local church move beyond empty religiosity to fully arrive at true saving faith.

ASSESSING UNDERSTANDING

You want to be fully certain your family, friends, and members of your faith community have trusted in Jesus for their salvation—and not fallen for some subtle counterfeit "gospel." I urge believers to let love lead them into beautiful yet sometimes difficult conversations about the Gospel. You can do this by asking people from your sphere of influence where they stand. Helpful questions in these important conversations include:

1. What does a person need to do to get to heaven?
2. How can a person have his or her sins forgiven?
3. Can a person lose his or her salvation, and if so, how?

4. To be saved, does a person need to do anything more than believe in Jesus?

5. If God said, "Say nothing but why you should get into heaven," how would you respond?

Ask these and similar questions and listen carefully. By now we should be able to discern what good answers to these questions should sound like, and identify subtle clues that would suggest a fundamental misunderstanding of the Gospel. Your conversations should be extensive enough for you to really get to the heart of what each person believes.

If you identify they do not provide evidence they understand the salvation-by-faith Gospel, or they are adding another false requirement to salvation other than Christ alone, then you must share the Gospel with them. Perhaps you are the only one equipped and able to reach these people in your sphere of influence, so you must not waver or delay in your responsibility. Through these clarifying conversations, God may use you to bring many people to faith throughout your lifetime.

FACING RESISTANCE

As you share the Gospel, you will undoubtedly face resistance—and particularly so with religious people who have bought into false "gospels." Some will not be ready to give up their self-righteousness, and they will push back. Others may accuse you of trying to teach people they have a "license to sin" (which you should counter by reminding them God desires obedience from His much-loved children, but not to obtain salvation).

Overall, you must strengthen yourself in God daily because you will likely face resistance as you try to rescue people. Remember, it is through believing the Gospel message that we obtain forgiveness of sins, reconciliation to God, full escape from the condemnation for sin, and an eternal home in heaven with the rest of God's family. No wonder the devil resists this Gospel so much and is hell-bent on keeping people from seeing this truth in all its beauty! Do not forget Jesus and His apostles also faced strong resistance for teaching the Gospel could be freely received as a gift. So be patient, pray for the people you speak with, and continue to voice the truth as the Holy Spirit leads you.

SAFEGUARDING OUR CHURCHES

Because the Gospel is the foundation for our salvation, there is nothing more critical than for us to protect the accurate representation of the Gospel in our churches. While many brilliant men and women teach the Bible and have much to offer, if a teacher gives evidence of teaching a counterfeit "gospel," we should not carelessly overlook this reality. The apostle Paul proclaimed: "But even if we or an angel from heaven should preach a gospel other than the one we preached to you, let them be under God's curse! As we have already said, so now I say again: If anybody is preaching to you a gospel other than what you accepted, let them be under God's curse!" (Galatians 1:8–9, NIV)

As difficult as it is, we cannot put up with teachers of a false "gospel"—even if 99 percent of what they offer us is of spectacular quality. No teacher—whether on television, in the pulpit, in books, audio teachings, or curricula—is worthy of addressing Jesus' faith community if they will present a message that leads them away from the Shepherd of our souls. Too much is at stake to allow our ears to hear a message that so dreadfully endangers our salvation. Paul knew this reality well, and he would not put up with it for a second. Regarding false "gospel" teachers who advocated salvation by works, Paul continued:

> This matter arose because some false believers had infiltrated our ranks to spy on the freedom we have in Christ Jesus and to make us slaves. We did not give in to them for a moment, so that the truth of the Gospel might be preserved for you. Galatians 2:4–5, NIV

Let us protect our churches and ourselves by allowing only those teachers who honor the Gospel as the Bible teaches it, making no exceptions. We cannot reach out the hand of cooperation to those who will undo our salvation any more than we should let the hands of those who commit abortions deliver our babies. We must guard the biblical purity of the most important message in the universe— the only message that can save.

MOVING FORWARD IN VICTORY

As we move forward, we should know we deliver this message with the full backing of the Lord. The authority of all authorities authorized us to deliver the message to every person in the world, commanding: "Go into all the world and preach the gospel to all creation" (Mark 16:15, NIV).

We do not go alone. Jesus told us we would have great help as we delivered His message. We read: "When you are brought before synagogues, rulers and authorities, do not worry about how you will defend yourselves or what you will say, for the Holy Spirit will teach you at that time what you should say" (Luke 12:11–12, NIV).

We can walk with confidence, knowing Jesus promised the gates of hell would not prevail against the Gospel. As we face various persecutions, we can remember God approves of the message and blesses us for carrying it forward. The Scriptures say, "How beautiful are the feet of those who bring good news!" (Romans 10:15, NIV) The message truly is beautiful, and so those who deliver the message do a beautiful thing—whether they are applauded or persecuted. We look forward to the day when Jesus says to us, "Well done, good and faithful servant!" (Matthew 25:23, NIV)

PERSONALLY TRUSTING IN JESUS

If any readers have not yet placed their trust in Jesus for their salvation, now is the right time to receive this gift of salvation. Consider what the God of the Universe has written in His Bible, what He has clearly called you to do in response to the reality of your sin, and the cure Jesus offers. Here's what God wants of you:

1. He tells you to believe Jesus died on the cross for you.
2. He tells you to formally accept Jesus as the Savior for your sins.
3. He tells you to reject all other attempts to get to heaven—including your self-righteousness.

If you are ready for this and haven't already called out to Jesus, pray the following prayer out loud:

"Jesus, I accept. I accept this offer of salvation You are extending to me. You can be my Savior, now and forever, and I know it. I quit my self-righteous attempts to get into heaven on my merits. I know doing good won't remove my guilt before God. I know trying to stop doing bad things won't remove the guilt from my past. I know You alone can take my guilt away, and so I accept You today. I believe You gave your life for me, taking my guilt and punishment upon yourself. You were guiltless, and I was guilty. Because You were punished in my place, I know my guilt has already been dealt with on the cross and I will never have to be punished. Thank You for doing this for me! I know You resurrected from the dead, proving You really were sent from God to take my sin away, and because of that amazing resurrection, I know I will get to see You someday. Jesus, thank You for winning my forgiveness, mediating my reconciliation to God, and preparing an eternal home in heaven for me. You are my Savior, and I trust in nothing other than You to save me. Amen."

If you have prayed this prayer sincerely before God, rejoice! You are saved! Now continue in this faith. On the words of God, you are saved. Yes, your sins are forgiven, you have been reconciled to God, and you have a place in heaven. Placing your trust in Jesus was the wisest thing you could ever do.

CONCLUSION

In closing, I'll leave you with a message from the apostle Paul that will encourage us to faithfully protect this Gospel we've spoken so much about:

Now I know that none of you among whom I have gone about preaching the kingdom will ever see me again. Therefore, I declare to you today that I am innocent of the blood of any of you. For I have not hesitated to proclaim to you the whole will of God. Keep watch over yourselves and all the flock of which the Holy Spirit has made you overseers. Be shepherds of the church of God, which he bought with his own blood. I know that after I leave, savage wolves will come in among you and will not spare the flock. Even from your own number men will arise and distort the truth in order to draw away disciples after them. So be on your guard! Remember that for three years I never stopped warning each of you night and day with tears. Now I commit you to God and to the word of his grace, which can build you up and give you an inheritance among all those who are sanctified.

Acts 20:25–32, NIV

Appendix A

SALVATION CREED

RECOMMENDED FOR CHURCHES

— *Appendix A* —

WE AFFIRM THE FOLLOWING SALVATION CREED

*Moreover, brethren, I declare to you the Gospel which
I preached to you, which also you received and in which you
stand, by which also you are saved, if you hold fast that word which
I preached to you—unless you believed in vain. For I delivered to you
first of all that which I also received: that Christ died for our sins
according to the Scriptures, and that He was buried, and that He
rose again the third day according to the Scriptures, and that
He was seen by Cephas, then by the twelve.*
1 Corinthians 15:1–5, NKJV

ALL HAVE SINNED: All human beings who live to the age where they know the difference between right and wrong choose to sin.

ONE SIN DAMNS: The guilt of one sin or more is enough to damn a person to eternal punishment on Judgment Day. If a believer in Jesus were ever to have one sin stick to his or her record after coming to faith in Jesus, it would be enough to damn that person to hell. Yet there is no condemnation for those who have faith in Jesus the Savior. Believers are fully forgiven.

DOING GOOD DOES NOT REMOVE GUILT: Doing good in the present does not remove guilt from past sins. Doing good plays no part in saving a person.

REFRAINING FROM EVIL DOES NOT REMOVE GUILT: Refraining from evil in the present does not remove guilt from past sins. Refraining from evil plays no part in saving a person.

SALVATION THROUGH JESUS' SACRIFICE: Nothing in the history of the universe has had the power to remove the guilt of even a single sin except for one Person through His one act: Jesus of Nazareth taking on the full guilt for the sins of the world and being punished fully unto death for those sins committed by others.

HIS RESURRECTION IS PROOF: Jesus' sin-atoning death saves us from our sins, and His miraculous bodily resurrection serves as proof that His substitutionary death was effectual to save us from our sins.

COMPLETE FORGIVENESS THROUGH FAITH: When a person believes Jesus took the full punishment for all his or her sin guilt when He gave His life on the cross, that person is fully forgiven.

FORGIVENESS OBTAINS RECONCILIATION FROM GOD: When a person is fully forgiven through faith in Jesus as Savior, he or she becomes legally "righteous" (free from all sin guilt) in God's eyes and is completely reconciled to Him.

NO CONDEMNATION FOR THE FORGIVEN: If a person becomes "righteous" in God's eyes and arrives at judgment day in such a state, there is nothing to be judged, condemned, and/or punished for.

SALVATION IS A GIFT: Forgiveness of sins and the consequent salvation is a gift obtained through faith in Jesus as Savior. One must do nothing other than accept Jesus as Savior by faith to obtain complete forgiveness of sins, reconciliation to God, and an eternal place in heaven.

FORSAKING SIN OUT OF GRATITUDE: All believers should forsake every sin in their lives. This is the reasonable service to the One who won their salvation at such a great price. However, it is important to always remember that obtaining Jesus' forgiveness is not contingent upon our choice to forsake sin.

DISCIPLINE FOR THE SINNING BELIEVER: While it is absolutely true that believers in Jesus do not lose their salvation when they sin, God has promised to treat believers as His children, and they can surely expect He will use His right to discipline them out of fatherly love when He deems it necessary—yet believers need not fear hell.

FORGIVENESS FOR PAST, PRESENT, AND FUTURE SINS: A believer in Jesus need not fear when they mess up, for Jesus already took the punishment for all their sins—past, present, and future.

ASSURANCE OF SALVATION: Assurance of salvation is the due inheritance of every believer from the moment they place their faith in Jesus as Savior. Believers in Jesus should feel the comfort of forgiveness and salvation as long as they trust in the Savior.

MAINTAINING SALVATION: The only requirement to maintain salvation after the first moment a believer trusts in Jesus as Savior is to continue on in that trust until death.

LOSING SALVATION: Salvation cannot be lost through sinful behavioral choices or lack of good works once it is obtained through faith in Jesus the Savior. However, salvation *can* be lost if the believer discontinues faith in Jesus and does not return to that faith. If the believer loses their faith but then returns to the original faith in Jesus the Savior, they will once again be within the safety of salvation. Salvation is obtained and maintained through faith in Jesus the

Savior, and that salvation may only be lost if a believer rejects faith in Jesus the Savior or is lead astray from that faith.

DEFINITION OF JUSTIFICATION: In the context of the salvation message (the Gospel), "justification" refers to the act whereby God declares a person righteous (sin-guilt free) when he or she puts trust in Jesus for salvation.

DEFINITION OF "REPENTANCE": In the context of the salvation message (the Gospel), "repentance" means "to change your mind" from unbelief in Jesus to belief in Him. In Acts 2:36–38 and Acts 3:17–20, Peter called his listeners to "repent" of their previous unbelief in Jesus and to turn to full faith in Jesus so that they could be forgiven of sins and obtain salvation.

THIS IS NOT "REPENTANCE": In the context of the salvation message (the Gospel) described in Acts 2:26–38 and 3:17–20, the requirement of "repentance" for salvation does *not* mean "to turn from all your sins." It is not true that we must turn away from all our sins to be saved, for no believer ever has or ever will turn away from all sin. To teach you must turn from all your sins to be saved by Jesus annuls faith, causes a person to turn to self-righteousness, and leads them astray from the true Gospel which teaches us to trust in Jesus alone for forgiveness and right standing with God.

ADDING WORKS TO FAITH MAKES SAVING FAITH INEFFECTUAL: If a person believes Jesus took the full punishment for all his or her sin guilt when He gave His life on the cross, yet then also adds the belief he or she must do good works to obtain and/or maintain salvation, the latter addition of reliance on good works will void the efficacy of the former faith. A partial faith in Jesus for salvation is no saving faith at all.

ADDING SELF-REFORMATION MAKES SAVING FAITH INEFFECTUAL: If a person believes Jesus took the full punishment for all his or her sin guilt when He gave His life on the cross, yet then also adds the belief he or she must stop doing sinful things (behavioral reformation) to obtain and/or maintain salvation, the latter addition of reliance on behavioral reformation will make void the efficacy of saving faith in Jesus. A partial faith in Jesus for salvation is no saving faith at all.

STAND FIRM: A person who has trusted in Jesus' sin-atoning work on the cross and believes in His victorious resurrection should stand firm in that faith, adding no other alleged requirements for salvation. First Corinthians 15:1–8 declares the Gospel (the salvation message) in the simplest and clearest of terms: "Moreover, brethren, I declare to you the Gospel which I preached to you, which also you received and in which you stand, by which also you are saved, if you hold fast that word which I preached to you—unless you believed in vain. For I delivered to you first of all that which I also received: that Christ died for our sins according to the Scriptures, and that He was buried, and that He rose again the third day according to the Scriptures, and that He was seen by Cephas, then by the twelve. After that He was seen by over five hundred brethren at once, of whom the greater part remain to the present, but some have fallen asleep. After that He was seen by James, then by all the apostles. Then last of all He was seen by me also, as by one born out of due time" (NKJV). We must believe this simple message, adding nothing to it, and taking nothing from it, and by this faith, we receive forgiveness of sins, reconciliation to God, and an eternal place in heaven.

For no one can lay any foundation other than the one already laid, which is Jesus Christ.
1 Corinthians 3:11, NIV

OVERVIEW OF
THE GOSPEL

— Appendix B —

OVERVIEW OF THE GOSPEL

THE GOSPEL IS the dead center bull's eye of our faith—that one and only message that has the power to change a person's eternal destination from hell to heaven. So, without further ado, here is an overview of the only Gospel message as the Bible teaches it and as God preaches it. If you believe it, trust it like you trust a sturdy chair, leaning back and putting all your weight on it, knowing it will catch your fall.

AN OVERVIEW OF THE INCREDIBLE STORY OF THE GOSPEL

OUR MISTREATMENT OF GOD. All human beings have committed a multitude of sin "crimes" throughout their life, and these sins go directly against the will and biblical law of God, the holy Creator of the Universe. This presents us with a massive problem because the uncomfortable truth is once a sinner commits a sin, he or she really has no ability to clear that sin off his or her record. Humans are mortal and are all destined to die, and the sin guilt we earned in this life makes death an absolutely hopeless situation. Why a hopeless situation? Because the Bible teaches we will continue to live after death and will be summoned to a court appearance before God, and we are *sinners*.

HELL WAS DESTINED TO BE OUR HOME. Each person has failed God's standards for heaven through their sinful choices on earth. The

Bible actually sets the standard for admission into heaven so incredibly high that *even one sin is too much sin for God*. This dreadful reality puts a somber reverence in our hearts toward the most holy and perfect God. With this said, we were certainly on our way to a "guilty" verdict. When a person is judged as guilty on their judgment day, they are refused admission into heaven and sent away from God's presence to the *hellish* lake of fire—an eternal place of dreadful punishment for sin in isolation from all the is good. Despite the jokes of popular humor, there will not be any parties bumping in this place. The sinner's fate is eternally sealed once the verdict comes out. We cannot change God's judgment.

GOD'S RESCUE MISSION. God was keenly aware of our hopeless situation, so in a great act of love and mercy, He sent a Savior to rescue us. Jesus came to earth on a mission to save people from the sin guilt that would earn them certain condemnation. Jesus humbled Himself by stepping down from His glorious place in heaven to visit earth, and He became a human to save humans. This Savior started out life on earth by being miraculously born as a human baby to a virgin young lady in the land of Israel. Jesus came to accomplish an act that would make it possible for sinners to have their sins *legally* and *justly* pardoned by God. If a sinner's sins are pardoned, there is no need for a "guilty" verdict, and without guilt, there is no need for punishment. God's incredible rescue mission would save sinners from the guilt, condemnation, and punishment they earned for themselves—a full escape!

A SWAP OF FATES. Here's how the rescue mission played out: Jesus grew from a baby to adulthood, living a completely sinless life. Because of His sinlessness, He didn't deserve any punishment for sin. Despite His innocence, Jesus willingly offered His life up to be punished for all the sin guilt we had earned through our sinful thoughts and actions so we wouldn't have to experience any punishment on judgment day. This amazing, God-ordained swap of fates took place on a single day and at a single event: *Jesus' death on the cross.*

A SUPPRISING CULMINATION: RESURRECTION. Jesus' lifeless body was laid in a tomb, cold and unresponsive. Most thought He was finished, never to be heard from again. Yet in a clash against the finality of all the deaths in history past, Jesus came back to life three days after being placed in the grave. This astonishing resurrection proved His mission was ordained by God and was fully satisfactory in His eyes.

ACTIVATING SALVATION. Today, God will lawfully forgive and clear the sin records of any individual on the planet if they will only accept Jesus as their personal Savior. It does not matter what they've done: *every single sin can be forgiven.* To activate God's free offer of forgiveness, all a person must do is say "yes" to the truth that Jesus' sacrificial death is enough to fully pardon sins and make a person right with God. God forgives a person's sins the instant a person receives this truth. Yes, it is this faith in Jesus that God requires of us, and when God sees our faith in the Savior He sent, He activates forgiveness in full. Concerning Jesus, "Salvation is found in no one else, for there is no other name under heaven given to mankind by which we must be saved" (Acts 4:12, NIV).

THE PRIZES. When a person is forgiven, he or she receives all kinds of amazing gifts from the God who came to the rescue. God gives a full pardon of sins to the forgiven person. A forgiven person also experiences reconciliation to God in such a way that he or she can begin an authentic friendship with God. And last but not least, the forgiven person receives an eternal place in God's family and an everlasting home in heaven. What an amazing and unexpected prize a saved sinner receives!

Appendix C

SALVATION VERSES OF THE NEW TESTAMENT

— *Appendix C* —

SALVATION VERSES OF THE NEW TESTAMENT

MATTHEW

Matthew 1:20–23 "But while he thought about these things, behold, an angel of the Lord appeared to him in a dream, saying, 'Joseph, son of David, do not be afraid to take to you Mary your wife, for that which is conceived in her is of the Holy Spirit. And she will bring forth a Son, and you shall call His name Jesus, for He will save His people from their sins.' So all this was done that it might be fulfilled which was spoken by the Lord through the prophet, saying: 'Behold, the virgin shall be with child, and bear a Son, and they shall call His name Immanuel,' which is translated, 'God with us.'"

Matthew 9:2 "Then behold, they brought to Him a paralytic lying on a bed. When Jesus say their faith, He said to the paralytic, 'Son, be of good cheer; your sins are forgiven you.'"

Matthew 20:28 "...[T]he Son of Man did not come to be served, but to serve, and to give His life a ransom for many."

Matthew 26:28 "For this is My blood of the new covenant, which is shed for many for the remission of sins."

Matthew 27:27–28:10 "Then the soldiers of the governor took Jesus into the Praetorium and gathered the whole garrison around Him. And they stripped Him and put a scarlet robe on Him. When they had twisted a crown of thorns, they put it on His head, and a reed in His right hand. And they bowed the knee before Him and mocked Him, saying, 'Hail, King of the Jews!' Then they spat on Him, and took the reed and struck Him on the head. And when they had mocked Him, they took the robe off Him, put His own clothes on Him, and led Him away to be crucified. Now as they came out, they found a man of Cyrene, Simon by name. Him they compelled to bear His cross. And when they had come to a place called Golgotha, that is to say, Place of a Skull, they gave Him sour wine mingled with gall to drink. But when He had tasted it, He would not drink. Then they crucified Him, and divided His garments, casting lots, that it might be fulfilled which was spoken by the prophet: 'They divided My garments among them, and for My clothing they cast lots.'... Then two robbers were crucified with Him, one on the right and another on the left. And those who passed by blasphemed Him, wagging their heads and saying, 'You who destroy the temple and build it in three days, save Yourself! If You are the Son of God, come down from the cross.' Likewise the chief priests also, mocking with the scribes and elders, said, 'He saved others; Himself He cannot save. If He is the King of Israel, let Him now come down from the cross, and we will believe Him. He trusted in God; let Him deliver Him now if He will have Him; for He said, "I am the Son of God."' Even the robbers who were crucified with Him reviled Him with the same thing. Now from the sixth hour until the ninth hour there was darkness over all the land. And about the ninth hour Jesus cried out with a loud voice, saying, 'Eli, Eli, lama sabachthani?' that is, 'My God, My God, why have You forsaken Me?' Some of those who stood there, when they heard that, said, 'This Man is calling for Elijah!' Immediately one of them ran and took a sponge, filled it with sour wine and put it on a reed, and offered it to Him to drink. The rest said, 'Let Him alone; let us see if Elijah will come to save Him.' And Jesus cried out again with a loud voice, and yielded up His spirit. Then, behold, the veil of the temple was torn in two from top to bottom; and the earth quaked, and the rocks were split, and the graves were opened; and many bodies of the saints who had fallen asleep were raised; and coming out of the graves after His resurrection, they went into the holy city and appeared to many. So when the centurion and those with him, who were guarding Jesus, saw the earthquake and the things that had happened, they feared greatly, saying, 'Truly this was the Son of God!' And many women who followed Jesus form Galilee, ministering to Him, were there looking on from afar, among whom were Mary Magdalene, Mary the mother of James and Joses, and the mother of Zebedee's sons. Now when evening had come, there came a rich man from Arimathea, named Joseph, who himself had also become a disciple of Jesus. This man went to Pilate and asked for the body of Jesus. Then Pilate commanded the body to be given to him. When Joseph had taken the body, he wrapped it in a clean linen cloth, and laid it in his new tomb which he had hewn out of the rock; and he rolled a large stone against the door of the tomb, and departed. And Mary Magdalene was there, and the other Mary, sitting opposite the tomb. On the next day, which followed the Day of Preparation, the chief priests and Pharisees gathered together to Pilate, saying, 'Sir, we remember, while He was still alive, how that deceiver said, "After three days I will rise." Therefore command that the tomb be made secure until the third day, lest His disciples come by night and steal Him away, and say to the people, "He has risen from the dead." So the last deception will be worse than the first.' Pilate said to them, 'You have a guard; go your way, make it as secure as you know how.' So they went and made the tomb secure, sealing the stone and setting the guard. Now after the Sabbath, as the first day of the week began to dawn, Mary Magdalene and the other Mary came to see the tomb. And behold, there was a great earthquake; for an angel of the Lord descended from heaven, and came and rolled back the stone from the door, and sat on it. His countenance was like lightening, and his clothing as white as snow. And the guards shook for fear of him, and became like dead men. But the angel answered and said to the women, 'Do not be afraid, for I know that you seek Jesus who was crucified. He is not here; for He is risen, as He said. Come, see the place where the Lord lay. And go quickly and tell His disciples that He is risen form the dead, and indeed He is going before you into Galilee; there you will see Him. Behold, I have told you.' So they went out quickly from the tomb with fear and great joy, and ran to bring His disciples word. And as they went to tell His disciples, behold, Jesus met them, saying, 'Rejoice!' So they came and held Him by the feet and worshiped Him. Then Jesus said to them, 'Do not be afraid. Go and tell My brethren to go to Galilee, and there they will see Me.'"

MARK

Mark 9:12b "...And how is it written concerning the Son of Man, that He must suffer many things and be treated with contempt?"

Mark 9:31 "For He taught His disciples and said to them, 'The Son of Man is being betrayed into the hands of men, and they will kill Him. And after He is killed, He will rise the third day.'"

Mark 10:33-34 "Behold, we are going up to Jerusalem, and the Son of Man will be betrayed to the chief priests and to the scribes; and they will condemn Him to death and deliver Him to the Gentiles; and they will mock Him, and scourge Him, and spit on Him, and kill Him. And the third day He will rise again."

Mark 14:24 "And He said to them, 'This is My blood of the new covenant which is shed for many.'"

Mark 15:16-16:14 "Then the soldiers led Him away into the hall called Praetorium, and they called together the whole garrison. And they clothed Him with purple; and they twisted a crown of thorns, put it on His head, and began to salute Him, 'Hail, King of the Jews!' Then they struck Him on the head with a reed and spat on Him; and bowing the knee, they worshiped Him. And when they had mocked Him, they took the purple off Him, put His own clothes on Him, and led Him out to crucify Him. Then they compelled a certain man, Simon a Cyrenian, the father of Alexander and Rufus, as he was coming out of the country and passing by, to bear His cross. And they brought Him to the place Golgotha, which is translated, Place of a Skull. Then they gave Him wine mingled with myrrh to drink, but He did not take it. And when they crucified Him, they divided His garments, casting lots for them to determine what every man should take. Now it was the third hour, and they crucified Him. And the inscription of

His accusation was written above: THE KING OF THE JEWS. With Him they also crucified two robbers, one on His right and the other on His left. So the Scripture was fulfilled which says, 'And He was numbered with the transgressors.' And those who passed by blasphemed Him, wagging their heads and saying, 'Aha! You who destroy the temple and build it in three days, save Yourself, and come down from the cross!' Likewise the chief priests also, mocking among themselves with the scribes, said, 'He saved others; Himself He cannot save. Let the Christ, the King of Israel, descend now from the cross, that we may see and believe.' Even those who were crucified with Him reviled Him. Now when the sixth hour had come, there was darkness over the whole land until the ninth hour. And at the ninth hour Jesus cried out with a loud voice, saying, 'Eloi, Eloi, lama sabachthani?' which is translated, 'My God, My God, why have You forsaken Me?' Some of those who stood by, when they head that, said, 'Look, He is calling for Elijah!' Then someone ran and filled a sponge full of sour wine, put it on a reed, and offered it to Him to drink, saying, 'Let Him alone; let us see if Elijah will come to take Him down.' And Jesus cried out with a loud voice, and breathed His last. Then the veil of the temple was torn in two from top to bottom. So when the centurion, who stood opposite Him, saw that He cried out like this and breathed His last, he said, 'Truly this man was the Son of God!' There were also women looking on from afar, among whom were Mary Magdalene, Mary the mother of James the Less and of Jones, and Salome, who also followed Him and ministered to Him when He was in Galilee, and many other women who came up with Him to Jerusalem. Now when evening had come, because it was the Preparation Day, that is, the day before the Sabbath, Joseph of Arimathea, a prominent council member, who was himself waiting for the kingdom of God, coming and taking courage, went in to Pilate and asked for the body of Jesus. Pilate marveled that He was already dead; and summoning the centurion, he asked him if He had been dead for some time. So when he found out from the centurion, he granted the body to Joseph. Then he bought fine linen, took Him down, and wrapped Him in the linen. And he laid Him in a tomb which had been hewn out of the rock, and rolled a stone against the door of the tomb. And Mary Magdalene and Mary the mother of Joses observed where He was laid. Now when the Sabbath was past, Mary Magdalene, Mary the mother of James, and Salome bought spices, that they might come and anoint Him. Very early in the morning, on the first day of the week, they came to the tomb when the sun had risen. And they said among themselves, 'Who will roll away the stone from the door of the tomb for us?' But when they looked up, they saw that the stone had been rolled away—for it was very large. And entering the tomb, they saw a young man clothed in a long white robe sitting on the right side; and they were alarmed. But he said to them, 'Do not be alarmed. You seek Jesus of Nazareth, who was crucified. He is risen! He is not here. See the place where they laid Him. But go, tell His disciples—and Peter—that He is going before you into Galilee; there you will see Him, as He said to you.' So they went out quickly and fled from the tomb, for they trembled and were amazed. And they said nothing to anyone, for they were afraid. Now when He rose early on the first day of the week, He

appeared first to Mary Magdalene, out of whom He had cast seven demons. She
went and told those who had been with Him, as they mourned and wept. And
when they heard that He was alive and had been seen by her, they did not believe.
After that, He appeared in another form to two of them as they walked and went
into the country. And they went and told it to the rest, but they did not believe
them either. Later He appeared to the eleven as they sat at the table; and He
rebuked their unbelief and hardness of heart, because they did not believe those
who had seen Him after He had risen."

Mark 16:15-16 "And He said to them, 'Go into all the world and preach the
gospel to every creature. He who believes and is baptized will be saved; but he
who does not believe will be condemned."

LUKE

Luke 1:76–79 "And you, child, will be called the prophet of the Highest; for
you will go before the face of the Lord to prepare His ways, to give knowledge of
salvation to His people by the remission of their sins, through the tender mercy of
our God, with which the Dayspring from on high has visited us; to give light to
those who sit in darkness and the shadow of death, to guide our feet into the way
of peace."

Luke 2:10-11 "Then the angel said to them, 'Do not be afraid, for behold, I
bring you good tidings of great joy which will be to all people. For there is born to
you this day in the city of David a Savior, who is Christ the Lord."

Luke 2:25–32 "And behold, there was a man in Jerusalem whose name was
Simeon, and this man was just and devout, waiting for the Consolation of Israel,
and the Holy Spirit was upon him. And it had been revealed to him by the Holy
Spirit that he would not see death before he had seen the Lord's Christ. So he
came by the Spirit into the temple. And when the parents brought in the Child
Jesus, to do for Him according to the custom of the law, he took Him up in his
arms and blessed God and said: 'Lord, now You are letting Your servant depart in
peace, according to Your word; for my eyes have seen your salvation which You
have prepared before the face of all peoples, a light to bring revelation to the
Gentiles, and the glory of Your people Israel.'"

Luke 4:16–21 "So He came to Nazareth, where He had been brought up. And
as His custom was, He went into the synagogue on the Sabbath day, and stood up
to read. And He was handed the book of the prophet Isaiah. And when He had
opened the book, He found the place where it was written: 'The Spirit of the Lord
is upon Me, because He has anointed Me to preach the gospel to the poor; He has
sent Me to heal the brokenhearted, to proclaim liberty to the captives and
recovery of sight to the blind, to set at liberty those who are oppressed; to

proclaim the acceptable year of the Lord.' Then He closed the book, and gave it back to the attendant and sat down. And the eyes of all who were in the synagogue were fixed on Him. And He began to say to them, 'Today this Scripture is fulfilled in your hearing.'"

Luke 5:23-25 "'Which is easier, to say, 'Your sins are forgiven you,' or to say, 'Rise up and walk'? But that you may know that the Son of Man has power on earth to forgive sins'—He said to the man who was paralyzed, 'I say to you, arise, take up your bed, and go to your house.' Immediately he rose up before them, took up what he had been lying on, and departed to his own house, glorifying God."

Luke 7:44-50 "Then He turned to the woman and said to Simon, 'Do you see this woman? I entered your house; you gave Me no water for My feet, but she has washed My feet with her tears and wiped them with the hair of her head. You gave Me no kiss, but this woman has not ceased to kiss My feet since the time I came in. You did not anoint My head with oil, but this woman has anointed My feet with fragrant oil. Therefore I say you, her sins, which are many, are forgiven, for she loved much. But to whom little is forgiven, the same loves little.' Then He said to her, 'Your sins are forgiven.' And those who sat at the table with Him began to say to themselves, 'Who is this who even forgives sins?' Then He said to the woman, 'Your faith has saved you. Go in peace.'"

Luke 8:11-13 "Now the parable is this: The seed is the word of God. Those by the wayside are the ones who hear; then the devil comes and takes away the word out of their hearts, lest they should believe and be saved. But the ones on the rock are those who, when they hear, receive the word with joy; and these have no root, who believe for a while and in time of temptation fall away."

Luke 9:22 "The Son of Man must suffer many things, and be rejected by the elders and chief priests and scribes, and be killed, and be raised the third day."

Luke 9:43-45 "And they were all amazed at the majesty of God. But while everyone marveled at all the things which Jesus did, He said to His disciples, 'Let these words sink down into your ears, for the Son of Man is about to be betrayed into the hands of men.' But they did not understand this saying, and it was hidden from them so that they did not perceive it; and they were afraid to ask Him about this saying."

Luke 9:51-56 "Now it came to pass, when the time had come for Him to be received up, that He steadfastly set His face to go to Jerusalem, and sent messengers before His face. And as they went, they entered a village of the Samaritans, to prepare for Him. But they did not receive Him, because His face was set for the journey to Jerusalem. And when His disciples James and John saw this, they said, 'Lord, do You want us to command fire to come down from heaven and consume them, just as Elijah did?' But He turned and rebuked them, and said, 'You do not know what manner of spirit you are of. For the Son of Man did not come to destroy men's lives but to save them.' And they went to another village."

Luke 18:31–33 "Then He took the twelve aside and said to them, 'Behold, we are going up to Jerusalem, and all things that are written by the prophets concerning the Son of Man will be accomplished. For He will be delivered to the Gentiles and will be mocked and insulted and spit upon. They will scourge Him and kill Him. And the third day He will rise again.'"

Luke 23:32–24:48 "There were also two others, criminals, led with Him to be put to death. And when they had come to the place called Calvary, there they crucified Him, and the criminals, one on the right hand and the other on the left. Then Jesus said, 'Father, forgive them, for they do not know what they do.' And they divided His garments and cast lots. And the people stood looking on. But even the rulers with them sneered, saying, 'He saved others, let Him save Himself if He is the Christ, the chosen of God.' The soldiers also mocked Him, coming and offering Him sour wine, and saying, 'If You are the King of the Jews, save Yourself.' And an inscription also was written over Him in letters of Greek, Latin, and Hebrew: THIS IS THE KING OF THE JEWS. Then one of the criminals who were hanged blasphemed Him, saying, 'If You are the Christ, save Yourself and us.' But the other, answering, rebuked him, saying, 'Do you not even fear God, seeing you are under the same condemnation? And we indeed justly, for we receive the due reward of our deeds; but this Man has done nothing wrong.' Then he said to Jesus, 'Lord, remember me when You come into Your kingdom.' And Jesus said to him, 'Assuredly, I say to you, today you will be with Me in Paradise.' Now it was about the sixth hour, and there was darkness over all the earth until the ninth hour. Then the sun was darkened, and the veil of the temple was torn in two. And when Jesus had cried out with a loud voice, He said, 'Father, into Your hands I commit My spirit.' Having said this, He breathed His last. So when the centurion saw what had happened, he glorified God, saying, 'Certainly this was a righteous Man!' And the whole crowd who came together to that sight, seeing what had been done, beat their breasts and returned. But all His acquaintances, and the women who followed Him from Galilee, stood at a distance, watching these things. Now behold, there was a man named Joseph, a council member, a good and just man. He had not consented to their decision and deed. He was home from Arimathea, a city of the Jews, who himself was also waiting for the kingdom of God. This man went to Pilate and asked for the body of Jesus. Then he took it down, wrapped it in linen, and laid it in a tomb that was hewn out of the rock, where no one had ever been lain before. That day was the Preparation, and the Sabbath drew near. And the women who had come with Him from Galilee followed after, and they observed the tomb and how His body was laid. Then they returned and prepared spices and fragrant oils. And they rested on the Sabbath according to the commandment. Now on the first day of the week, very early in the morning, they, and certain other women with them, came to the tomb bringing the spices which they had prepared. But they found the stone rolled away from the tomb. Then they went in and did not find the body of the Lord Jesus. And it happened, as they were greatly perplexed about this, that behold, two men stood by them in shining garments. Then, as they were afraid and bowed their faces to the earth, they said to them, 'Why do you seek the living among the dead? He is not here, but is risen! Remember how He spoke to you when He was still in Galilee, saying, 'The Son of Man must be delivered into the hands of sinful men, and be crucified, and the third day rise again.' And they remembered His words. Then they returned from the tomb and told all these things to the eleven and to all the rest. It was Mary Magdalene, Joanna, Mary the mother of James, and the other women with them, who told these things to the apostles. And their words seemed to them like idle tales, and they did not believe them. But Peter arose and ran to the tomb; and stooping down, he saw the linen cloths lying by themselves; and he departed, marveling to himself at what had happened. Now behold, two of them were traveling that same day to a village called Emmaus, which was seven miles from Jerusalem. And they talked together of all these things which had happened. So it was, while they conversed and reasoned, that Jesus Himself drew near and went with them. But their eyes were restrained, so that they did not know Him. And He said to them, 'What kind of conversation is this that you have with one another as you walk and are sad?' Then the one whose name was Cleopas answered and said to Him, 'Are You the only stranger in Jerusalem, and have You not known the things which happened there in these days?' And He said to them, 'What things?' So they said to Him, 'The things concerning Jesus of Nazareth, who was a Prophet mighty in deed and word before God and all the people, and how the chief priests and our rulers delivered Him to be condemned to death, and crucified Him. But we were hoping that it was He who was going to redeem Israel. Indeed, besides all this, today is the third day since these things happened. Yes, and certain women of our company, who arrived at the tomb early, astonished us. When they did not find His body, they came saying that they had also seen a vision of angels who said He was alive. And certain of those who were with us went to the tomb and found it just as the women had said; but Him they did not see. Then He said to them, 'O foolish ones, and slow of heart to believe in all that the prophets have spoken! Ought not the Christ to have suffered these things and to enter into His glory?' And beginning at Moses and all the Prophets, He expounded to them in all the Scriptures the things concerning Himself. Then they drew near to the village where they were going, and He indicated that He would have gone farther. But they constrained Him, saying, 'Abide with us, for it is toward evening, and the day is far spent.' And He went in to stay with them. Now it came to pass, as He sat at the table with them, that He took bread, blessed and broke it, and gave it to them. Then their eyes were opened and they knew Him; and He vanished from their sight. And they said to one another, 'Did not our heart burn within us while He talked with us on the road, and while He opened the Scriptures to us?' So they rose up that very hour and returned to Jerusalem, and found the eleven and those who were with them gathered together, saying, 'The Lord is risen indeed, and has appeared to Simon!' And they told about the things that had happened on the road, and how He was known to them in the breaking of bread. Now as they said these things, Jesus Himself stood in the midst of them, and said to them, 'Peace to you.' But they were terrified and frightened, and supposed they had seen a spirit. And He said to them, 'Why are you troubled? And why do doubts arise in your hearts? Behold My hands and My feet, that it is I Myself. Handle Me and see, for a spirit does not have flesh and bones as you see I have.' When He had said this, He showed them His hands and His feet. But while they still did not believe for joy, and marveled, He said to them, 'Have you any food here?' So they gave Him a piece of a broiled fish and some honeycomb. And He took it and ate in their presence. Then He said to them, 'These are the words which I spoke to you while I was still with you, that all things must be fulfilled which were written in the Law of Moses and the Prophets and the Psalms concerning Me.' And He opened their understanding, that they might comprehend the Scriptures. Then He said to them, 'Thus it is written, and thus it was necessary for the Christ to suffer and to rise from the dead the third day, and that repentance and remission of sins should be preached in His name to all nations, beginning at Jerusalem. And you are witnesses of these things."

JOHN

John 1:12–13 "But as many as received Him, to them He gave the right to become children of God, to those who believe in His name: who were born, not of blood, nor of the will of the flesh, nor of the will of man, but of God."

John 1:29 "The next day John saw Jesus coming toward him, and said, 'Behold! The Lamb of God who takes away the sin of the world!'"

John 3:14–18 "And as Moses lifted up the serpent in the wilderness, even so must the Son of Man be lifted up, that whoever believes in Him should not perish but have eternal life. For God so loved the world that He gave His only begotten Son, that whoever believes in Him should not perish but have everlasting life. For God did not send His Son into the world to condemn the world, but that the world through Him might be saved. He who believes in Him is not condemned; but he who does not believe is condemned already, because he has not believed in the name of the only begotten Son of God."

John 3:36 "He who believes in the Son has everlasting life; and he who does not believe the Son shall not see life, but the wrath of God abides on Him."

John 4:25–26 "The woman said to Him, 'I know that Messiah is coming' (who is called Christ). 'When He comes, He will tell us all things.' Jesus said to her, 'I who speak to you am He."

John 5:24 "Most assuredly, I say to you, he who hears My word and believes in Him who sent Me has everlasting life, and shall not come into judgment, but has passed from death into life."

John 6:28–29 "Then they said to Him, 'What shall we do, that we may work the works of God?' Jesus answered and said to them, 'This is the work of God, that you believe in Him whom He sent.'"

John 6:40 "And this is the will of Him who sent Me, that everyone who sees the Son and believes in Him may have everlasting life; and I will raise him up at the last day."

John 6:47–58 "'Most assuredly, I say to you, he who believes in Me has everlasting life. I am the bread of life. Your fathers ate the manna in the wilderness, and are dead. This is the bread which comes down from heaven, that one may eat of it and not die. I am the living bread which came down from heaven. If anyone eats of this bread, he will live forever; and the bread that I shall give is My flesh, which I shall give for the life of the world.' The Jews therefore quarreled among themselves, saying, 'How can this Man give us His flesh to eat?' Then Jesus said to them, 'Most assuredly, I say to you, unless you eat the flesh of the Son of Man and drink His blood, you have no life in you. Whoever eats My flesh and drinks My blood has eternal life, and I will raise him up at the last day. For My flesh is food indeed, and My blood is drink indeed. He who eats My flesh and drinks My blood abides in Me, and I in him. As the living Father sent Me, and I live because of the Father, so he who feeds on Me will live because of Me. This is the bread which came down from heaven—not as your fathers ate the manna, and are dead. He who eats this bread will live forever.'"

John 6:66–69 "From that time many of His disciples went back and walked with Him no more. Then Jesus said to the twelve, 'Do you also want to go away?' But Simon Peter answered Him, 'Lord, to whom shall we go? You have the words of eternal life. Also we have come to believe and know that You are the Christ, the Son of the living God.'"

John 8:24 "Therefore I said to you that you will die in your sins; for if you do not believe that I am He, you will die in your sins."

John 8:36 "Therefore if the Son makes you free, you are free indeed."

John 10:9–18 "I am the door. If anyone enters by Me, he will be saved, and will go in and out and find pasture. The thief does not come except to steal, and to kill, and to destroy. I have come that they may have life, and that they may have it more abundantly. I am the good shepherd. The good shepherd gives His life for the sheep. But a hireling, he who is not the shepherd, one who does not own the sheep, sees the wolf coming and leaves the sheep and flees; and the wolf catches the sheep and scatters them. The hireling flees because he is a hireling and does not care about the sheep. I am the good shepherd; and I know My sheep, and am known by My own. As the Father knows Me, even so I know the Father; and I lay down My life for the sheep. And other sheep I have which are not of this fold; them also I must bring, and they will hear My voice; and there will be one flock and one shepherd. Therefore My Father loves Me, because I lay down My life that I may take it again. No one takes it from Me, but I lay it down of Myself. I have power to lay it down, and I have power to take it again. This command I have received form My Father."

John 10:27–28 "My sheep hear My voice, and I know them, and they follow Me. And I give them eternal life, and they shall never perish; neither shall anyone snatch them out of My hand."

John 11:25–26 "I am the resurrection and the life. He who believes in Me, though he may die, he shall live. And whoever lives and believes in Me shall never die. Do you believe this?"

John 12:31-32 "Now is the judgment of this world; now the ruler of this world will be cast out. And I, if I am lifted up from the earth, will draw all peoples to Myself."

John 14:6 "I am the way, the truth, and the life. No one comes to the Father except through Me."

John 16:26–27 "In that day you will ask in My name, and I do not say to you that I shall pray the Father for you; for the Father Himself loves you, because you have loved Me, and have believed that I came forth from God."

John 17:1-3 Jesus spoke these words, lifted up His eyes to heaven, and said: 'Father, the hour has come. Glorify You Son, that Your Son also may glorify You, as You have given Him authority over all flesh, that He should give eternal life to as many as You have given Him. And this is eternal life, that they may know You, the only true God, and Jesus Christ whom You have sent."

John 19:16–21:14 "Then he delivered Him to them to be crucified. So they took Jesus and led Him away. And He, bearing His cross, went out to a place called *the Place of a Skull*, which is called is Hebrew, Golgotha, where they crucified Him, and two others with Him, one on either side, and Jesus in the center. Now Pilate wrote a title and put it on the cross. And the writing was: JESUS OF NAZARETH, THE KING OF THE JEWS. Then many of the Jews read this title, for the place where Jesus was crucified was near the city; and it was written in Hebrew, Greek, and Latin. Therefore the chief priests of the Jews said to Pilate, 'Do not write, "The King of the Jews," but, "He said, 'I am the King of the Jews.'"' Pilate answered, 'What I have written, I have written.' Then the soldiers, when they had crucified Jesus, took His garments and made four parts, to each soldier a part, and also the tunic. Now the tunic was without seam, woven from the top in one piece. They said therefore among themselves, 'Let us not tear it, but cast lots for it, whose it shall be,' that the Scripture might be fulfilled which says: 'They divided My garments among them, and for My clothing they cast lots.'" Therefore the soldiers did these things. Now there stood by the cross of Jesus His mother, and His mother's sister, Mary the wife of Clopas, and Mary Magdalene. When Jesus therefore saw His mother, and the disciple whom He loved standing by, He said to His mother, 'Woman, behold your son!' Then He said to the disciple, 'Behold your mother!' And from that hour that disciple took her to his own home. After this, Jesus, knowing that all things were now accomplished, that the Scripture might be fulfilled, said, 'I thirst!' Now a vessel full of sour wine was sitting there; and they filled a sponge with sour wine, put it on hyssop, and put it to His mouth. So when Jesus had received the sour wine, He said, 'It is finished!' And bowing His head, He gave up His spirit. Therefore, because it was the Preparation Day, that the bodies should not remain on the cross on the Sabbath (for that Sabbath was a high day), the Jews asked Pilate that their legs might be broken, and that they might be taken away. Then the soldiers came and broke the legs of the first and of the other who was crucified with Him. But when they came to Jesus and saw that He was already dead, they did not break His legs. But one of the soldiers pierced His side with a spear, and immediately blood and water came out. And he who has seen has testified, and his testimony is true; and he knows that he is telling the truth, so that you may believe. For these things were done that the Scripture should be fulfilled, 'Not one of His bones shall be broken.' And again another Scripture says, 'They shall look on Him whom they pierced.' And he, stooping down and looking in, saw the linen cloths lying there; yet he did not go in. Then Simon Peter came, following him, and went into the tomb; and he saw the linen cloths lying there, and the handkerchief that had been around His head, not lying with the linen cloths, but folded together in a place by itself. Then the other disciple, who came to the tomb first, went in also; and he saw and believed. For as yet they did not know the Scripture, that He must rise again from the dead. Then the disciples went away again to their own homes. But Mary stood outside by the tomb weeping, and as she wept she stooped down and looked into the tomb. And she saw two angels in white sitting, one at the head and the other at the feet, where the body of Jesus had lain. Then they said to her, 'Woman, why are you weeping?' She said to them, 'Because they have taken away my Lord, and I do not know where they have laid Him.' Now when she said this, she turned around and saw Jesus standing there, and did not know that it was Jesus. Jesus said to her, 'Woman, why are you weeping? Whom are you seeking?' She, supposing Him to be the gardener, said to Him, 'Sir, if You have carried Him away, tell me where You have laid Him, and I will take Him away.' Jesus said to her, 'Mary!' She turned and said to Him, 'Rabboni!' (which is to say, Teacher). Jesus said to her, 'Do not cling to Me, for I have not yet ascended to My Father; but go to My brethren and say to them, 'I am ascending to My Father and your Father, and to My God and your God.' Mary Magdalene came and told the disciples that she had seen the Lord, and that He had spoken these things to her. Then, the same day at evening, being the first day of the week, when the doors were shut where the disciples were assembled, for fear of the Jews, Jesus came and stood in the midst, and said to them, 'Peace be with you.' When He had said this, He showed them His hands and His side. Then the disciples were glad when they saw the Lord. So Jesus said to them again, 'Peace to you! As the Father has sent Me, I also send you.' And when He had said this, He breathed on them, and said to them, 'Receive the Holy Spirit. If you forgive the sins of any, they are forgiven them; if you retain the sins of any, they are retained.' Now Thomas, called the Twin, one of the twelve, was not with them when Jesus came. The other disciples therefore said to him, 'We have seen the Lord.' So he said to them, 'Unless I see in His hands the print of the nails, and put my finger into the print of the nails, and put my hand into His side, I will not believe.' And after eight days His disciples were again inside, and Thomas with them. Jesus came, the doors being shut, and stood in the midst, and said, 'Peace to you!' Then He said to Thomas, 'Reach your finger here, and look at My hands; and reach your hand here, and put it into My side. Do not be unbelieving, but believing.' And Thomas answered and said to Him, 'My Lord and my God!' Jesus said to him, 'Thomas, because you have seen Me, you have believed. Blessed are those who have not seen and yet have believed.' And truly Jesus did many other signs in the presence of His disciples, which are not written in this book; but these are written that you may believe that Jesus is the Christ, the Son of God, and that believing you may have life in His name. After these things Jesus showed Himself again to the disciples at the Sea of Tiberias, and in this way He showed Himself: Simon Peter, Thomas called the Twin, Nathanael of Cana in Galilee, the sons of Zebedee, and two others of His disciples were together. Simon Peter said to them, 'I am going fishing.' They said to him, 'We are going with you also.' They went out and immediately got into the boat, and that night they caught nothing. But when the morning had now come, Jesus stood on the shore; yet the disciples did not know that it was Jesus. Then Jesus said to them, 'Children, have you any food?' They answered Him, 'No.' And He said to them, 'Cast the net on the right side of the boat, and you will find some.' So they cast, and now they were not able to draw it in because of the multitude of fish. Therefore that disciple whom Jesus loved said to Peter, 'It is the Lord!' Now when Simon Peter heard that it was the Lord, he put on his outer garment (for he had removed it), and plunged into the sea. But the other disciples came in the little boat (for they were not far from land, but about two hundred cubits), dragging the net with fish. Then, as soon as they had come to land, they saw a fire of coals there, and fish laid on it, and bread. Jesus said to them, 'Bring some of the fish which you have just caught.' Simon Peter went up and dragged the net to land, full of large fish, one hundred and fifty-three; and although there were so many, the net was not broken. Jesus said to them, 'Come and eat breakfast.' Yet none of the disciples dared ask Him, 'Who are You?'—knowing that it was the Lord. Jesus then came and took the bread and gave it to them, and likewise the fish. This is now the third time Jesus showed Himself to His disciples after He was raised from the dead."

ACTS

Acts 2:21 "And it shall come to pass that whoever calls on the name of the Lord Shall be saved."

Acts 2:22-36 "Men of Israel, hear these words: Jesus of Nazareth, a Man attested by God to you by miracles, wonders, and signs which God did through Him in your midst, as you yourselves also know—Him, being delivered by the determined purpose and foreknowledge of God, you have taken by lawless hands, have crucified, and put to death; whom God raised up, having loosed the pains of death, because it was not possible that He should be held by it. For David says concerning Him: 'I foresaw the Lord always before my face, for He is at my right hand, that I may not be shaken. Therefore my heart rejoiced, and my tongue was glad; Moreover my flesh also will rest in hope. For You will not leave my soul in Hades, nor will You allow Your Holy One to see corruption. You have made known to me the ways of life; You will make me full of joy in Your presence.' Men and brethren, let me speak freely to you of the patriarch David, that he is both dead and buried, and his tomb is with us to this day. Therefore, being a prophet, and knowing that God had sworn with an oath to him that of the fruit of his body, according to the flesh, He would raise up the Christ to sit on his throne, he, foreseeing this, spoke concerning the resurrection of the Christ, that His soul was not left in Hades, nor did His flesh see corruption. This Jesus God has raised up, of which we are all witnesses. Therefore being exalted to the right hand of God, and having received from the Father the promise of the Holy Spirit, He poured out this which you now see and hear. For David did not ascend into the heavens, but he says himself: 'The Lord said to my Lord, "Sit at My right hand, Till I make Your enemies Your footstool."' Therefore let all the house of Israel know assuredly that God has made this Jesus, whom you crucified, both Lord and Christ."

Acts 2:38-39 "Then Peter said to them, 'Repent, and let every one of you be baptized in the name of Jesus Christ for the remission of sins; and you shall receive the gift of the Holy Spirit. For the promise is to you and to your children, and to all who are afar off, as many as the Lord our God will call."

Acts 3:18-19 "But those things which God foretold by the mouth of all His prophets, that the Christ would suffer, He has thus fulfilled. Repent therefore and be converted, that your sins may be blotted out, so that times of refreshing may come from the presence of the Lord..."

Acts 4:8–12 "Then Peter, filled with the Holy Spirit, said to them, 'Rulers of the people and elders of Israel: If we this day are judged for a good deed done to a helpless man, by what means he has been made well, let it be known to you all, and to all the people of Israel, that by the name of Jesus Christ of Nazareth, whom you crucified, whom God raised from the dead, by Him this man stands here before you whole. This is the "stone which was rejected by you builders, which has become the chief cornerstone." Nor is there salvation in any other, for there is no other name under heaven given among men by which we must be saved."

Acts 8:29–37 "Then the Spirit said to Philip, 'Go near and overtake this chariot.' So Philip ran to him, and heard him reading the prophet Isaiah, and said, 'Do you understand what you are reading?' And he said, 'How can I, unless someone guides me?' And he asked Philip to come up and sit with him. The place in the Scripture which he read was this: 'He was led as a sheep to the slaughter; and as a lamb before its shearer is silent, so He opened not His mouth. In His humiliation His justice was taken away, and who will declare His generation? For His life is taken from the earth.' So the eunuch answered Philip and said, 'I ask you, of whom does the prophet say this, of himself or of some other man?' Then Philip opened his mouth, and beginning at this Scripture, preached Jesus to him. Now as they went down the road, they came to some water. And the eunuch said, 'See, here is water. What hinders me from being baptized?' Then Philip said, 'If you believe with all your heart, you may.' And he answered and said, 'I believe that Jesus Christ is the Son of God.'"

Acts 10:34–48 "Then Peter opened his mouth and said: 'In truth I perceive that God shows no partiality. But in every nation whoever fears Him and works righteousness is accepted by Him. The word which God sent to the children of Israel, preaching peace through Jesus Christ—He is Lord of all—that word you know, which was proclaimed throughout all Judea, and began from Galilee after the baptism which John preached: how God anointed Jesus of Nazareth with the Holy Spirit and with power, who went about doing good and healing all who were oppressed by the devil, for God was with Him. And we are witnesses of all things which He did both in the land of the Jews and in Jerusalem, whom they killed by hanging on a tree. Him God raised up on the third day, and showed Him openly, not to all the people, but to witnesses chosen before by God, even to us who ate and drank with Him after He arose from the dead. And He commanded us to preach to the people, and to testify that it is He who was ordained by God to be Judge of the living and the dead. To Him all the prophets witness that, through His name, whoever believes in Him will receive remission of sins.' While Peter was still speaking these words, the Holy Spirit fell upon all those who heard the word. And those of the circumcision who believed were astonished, as many as came with Peter, because the gift of the Holy Spirit had been poured out on the Gentiles also. For they heard them speak with tongues and magnify God. Then Peter answered, 'Can anyone forbid water, that these should not be baptized who have received the Holy Spirit just as we have?' And he commanded them to be baptized in the name of the Lord. Then they asked him to stay a few days."

Acts 11:17 "If therefore God gave them the same gift as He gave us when we believed on the Lord Jesus Christ, who was I that I could withstand God?"

Acts 13:26–39 "Men and brethren, sons of the family of Abraham, and those among you who fear God, to you the word of this salvation has been sent. For those who dwell in Jerusalem, and their rulers, because they did not know Him, nor even the voices of the Prophets which are read every Sabbath, have fulfilled them in condemning Him. And though they found no cause for death in Him, they asked Pilate that He should be put to death. Now when they had fulfilled all that was written concerning Him, they took Him down from the tree and laid Him in a tomb. But God raised Him from the dead. He was seen for many days by those who came up with Him from Galilee to Jerusalem, who are His witnesses to the people. And we declare to you glad tidings—that promise which was made to the fathers. God has fulfilled this for us their children, in that He has raised up Jesus. As it is also written in the second Psalm: 'You are My Son, today I have begotten You.' And that He raised Him from the dead, no more to return to corruption, He has spoken thus: 'I will give you the sure mercies of David.' Therefore He also says in another Psalm: 'You will not allow Your Holy One to see corruption.' For David, after he had served his own generation by the will of God, fell asleep, was buried with his fathers, and saw corruption; but He whom God raised up saw no corruption. Therefore let it be known to you, brethren, that through this Man is preached to you the forgiveness of sins; and by Him everyone who believes is justified from all things from which you could not be justified by the law of Moses."

Acts 15:7–11 "And when there had been much dispute, Peter rose up and said to them: 'Men and brethren, you know that a good while ago God chose among us, that by my mouth the Gentiles should hear the word of the gospel and believe. So God, who knows the heart, acknowledged them by giving them the Holy Spirit, just as He did to us, and made no distinction between us and them, purifying their hearts by faith. Now therefore, why do you test God by putting a yoke on the neck of the disciples which neither our fathers nor we were able to bear? But we believe that through the grace of the Lord Jesus Christ we shall be saved in the same manner as they."

Acts 16:30–31 "And he brought them out and said, 'Sirs, what must I do to be saved?' So they said, 'Believe on the Lord Jesus Christ, and you will be saved, you and your household.'"

Acts 22:16 "And now why are you waiting? Arise and be baptized, and wash away your sins, calling on the name of the Lord."

Acts 26:18 "[T]o open their eyes, in order to turn them from darkness to light, and from the power of Satan to God, that they may receive forgiveness of sins and an inheritance among those who are sanctified by faith in Me."

ROMANS

Romans 1:16 "For I am not ashamed of the gospel of Christ, for it is the power of God to salvation for everyone who believes..."

Romans 3:21-28 "But now the righteousness of God apart from the law is revealed, being witnessed by the Law and the Prophets, even the righteousness of God, through faith in Jesus Christ, to all and on all who believe. For there is no difference; for all have sinned and fall short of the glory of God, being justified freely by His grace through the redemption that is in Christ Jesus, whom God set forth as a propitiation by His blood, through faith, to demonstrate His righteousness, because in His forbearance God had passed over the sins that were previously committed, to demonstrate at the present time His righteousness, that He might be just and the justifier of the one who has faith in Jesus. Where is boasting then? It is excluded. By what law? Of works? No, but by the law of faith. Therefore we conclude that a man is justified by faith apart from the deeds of the law."

Romans 4:5 "But to him who does not work but believes on Him who justifies the ungodly, his faith is accounted for righteousness..."

Romans 5:1-2 "Therefore, having been justified by faith, we have peace with God through our Lord Jesus Christ, through whom also we have access by faith into this grace in which we stand, and rejoice in hope of the glory of God."

Romans 5:8-9 "But God demonstrates His own love toward us, in that while we were still sinners, Christ died for us. Much more then, having now been justified by His blood, we shall be saved from wrath through Him."

Romans 5:11 "... [B]ut we also rejoice in God through our Lord Jesus Christ, through whom we have now received the reconciliation."

Romans 5:15-16 "But the gift is not like the offense. For if by the one man's offense many died, much more the grace of God and the gift by the grace of the one Man, Jesus Christ, abounded to many. And the gift is not like that which came through the one who sinned. For the judgment which came from one offense resulted in condemnation, but the free gift which came from many offenses resulted in justification."

Romans 8:3–4 "For what the law could not do in that it was weak through the flesh, God did by sending His own Son in the likeness of sinful flesh, on account of sin: He condemned sin in the flesh, that the righteous requirement of the law might be fulfilled in us who do not walk according to the flesh but according to the Spirit."

Romans 8:33–34 "Who shall bring a charge against God's elect? It is God who justifies. Who is he who condemns? It is Christ who died, and furthermore is also risen, who is even at the right hand of God, who also makes intercession for us."

Romans 9:30–32 "What shall we say then? That Gentiles, who did not pursue righteousness, have attained to righteousness, even the righteousness of faith; but Israel, pursuing the law of righteousness, has not attained to the law of righteousness. Why? Because they did not seek it by faith, but as it were, by the works of the law…"

Romans 10:3–4 "For they being ignorant of God's righteousness, and seeking to establish their own righteousness, have not submitted to the righteousness of God. For Christ is the end of the law for righteousness to everyone who believes."

Romans 10:8–11 "But what does it say? 'The word is near you, in your mouth and in your heart' (that is, the word of faith which we preach): that if you confess with your mouth the Lord Jesus and believe in your heart that God has raised Him from the dead, you will be saved. For with the heart one believes unto righteousness, and with the mouth confession is made unto salvation. For the Scripture says, 'Whoever believes on Him will not be put to shame.'"

Romans 10:13 "For 'whoever calls on the name of the Lord shall be saved.'"

1 CORINTHIANS

1 Corinthians 15:1–4 "Moreover, brethren, I declare to you the gospel which I preached to you, which also you received and in which you stand, by which also you are saved, if you hold fast that word which I preached to you—unless you believed in vain. For I delivered to you first of all that which I also received: that Christ died for our sins according to the Scriptures, and that He was buried, and that He rose again the third day according to the Scriptures…"

2 CORINTHIANS

2 Corinthians 5:18–21 "Now all things are of God, who has reconciled us to Himself through Jesus Christ, and has given us the ministry of reconciliation, that is, that God was in Christ reconciling the world to Himself, not imputing their trespasses to them, and has committed to us the word of reconciliation. Now then, we are ambassadors for Christ, as though God were pleading through us: we implore you on Christ's behalf, be reconciled to God. For He made Him who knew no sin to be sin for us, that we might become the righteousness of God in Him."

GALATIANS

Galatians 2:16 "...[K]nowing that a man is not justified by the works of the law but by faith in Jesus Christ, even we have believed in Christ Jesus, that we might be justified by faith in Christ and not by the works of the law; for by the works of the law no flesh shall be justified."

Galatians 3:13 "Christ has redeemed us from the curse of the law, having become a curse for us (for it is written, 'Cursed is everyone who hangs on a tree')..."

Galatians 3:26 "For you are all sons of God through faith in Christ Jesus."

Galatians 4:4-5 "But when the fullness of the time had come, God sent forth His Son, born of a woman, born under the law, to redeem those who were under the law, that we might receive the adoption as sons."

EPHESIANS

Ephesians 1:7 "In Him we have redemption through His blood, the forgiveness of sins, according to the riches of His grace..."

Ephesians 1:13 "In Him you also trusted, after you heard the word of truth, the gospel of your salvation; in whom also, having believed, you were sealed with the Holy Spirit of promise..."

Ephesians 2:8-9 "For by grace you have been saved through faith, and that not of yourselves; it is the gift of God, not of works, lest anyone should boast."

Ephesians 2:13 "But now in Christ Jesus you who once were far off have been brought near by the blood of Christ."

Ephesians 4:32 "And be kind to one another, tenderhearted, forgiving one another, even as God in Christ forgave you."

Ephesians 5:2 "And walk in love, as Christ also has loved us and given Himself for us, an offering and a sacrifice to God for a sweet-smelling aroma."

PHILIPPIANS

Philippians 3:8–9 "Yet indeed I also count all things loss for the excellence of the knowledge of Christ Jesus my Lord, for whom I have suffered the loss of all things, and count them as rubbish, that I may gain Christ and be found in Him, not having my own righteousness, which is from the law, but that which is through faith in Christ, the righteousness which is from God by faith…"

COLOSSIANS

Colossians 1:13–14 "He has delivered us from the power of darkness and conveyed us into the kingdom of the Son of His love, in whom we have redemption through His blood, the forgiveness of sins."

Colossians 1:19–23a "For it pleased the Father that in Him all the fullness should dwell, and by Him to reconcile all things to Himself, by Him, whether things on earth or things in heaven, having made peace through the blood of His cross. And you, who once were alienated and enemies in your mind by wicked works, yet now He has reconciled in the body of His flesh through death, to present you holy, and blameless, and above reproach in His sight—if indeed you continue in the faith, grounded and steadfast, and are not moved away from the hope of the gospel which you heard…"

Colossians 2:13–14 "And you, being dead in your trespasses and the uncircumcision of your flesh, He has made alive together with Him, having forgiven you all trespasses, having wiped out he handwriting of requirements that was against us, which was contrary to us. And He has taken it out of the way, having nailed it to the cross."

1 TIMOTHY

1 Timothy 1:15–16 "This is a faithful saying and worthy of all acceptance, that Christ Jesus came into the world to save sinners, of whom I am chief. However, for this reason I obtained mercy, that in me first Jesus Christ might show all longsuffering, as a pattern to those who are going to believe on Him for everlasting life."

1 Timothy 2:5–6a "For there is one God and one Mediator between God and men, the Man Christ Jesus, who gave Himself a ransom for all…"

2 TIMOTHY

2 Timothy 2:8 "Remember that Jesus Christ, of the seed of David, was raised from the dead according to my gospel..."

TITUS

Titus 2:13–14a "...[L]ooking for the blessed hope and glorious appearing of our great God and Savior Jesus Christ, who gave Himself for us, that He might redeem us from every lawless deed and purify for Himself His own special people..."

Titus 3:4–7 "But when the kindness and the love of God our Savior toward man appeared, not by works of righteousness which we have done, but according to His mercy He saved us, through the washing of regeneration and renewing of the Holy Spirit, whom He poured out on us abundantly though Jesus Christ our Savior, that having been justified by His grace we should become heirs according to the hope of eternal life."

HEBREWS

Hebrews 9:11–15 "But Christ came as High Priest of the good things to come, with the greater and more perfect tabernacle not made with hands, that is, not of this creation. Not with the blood of goats and calves, but with His own blood He entered the Most Holy Place once for all, having obtained eternal redemption. For if the blood of bulls and goats and the ashes of a heifer, sprinkling the unclean, sanctifies for the purifying of the flesh, how much more shall the blood of Christ, who through the eternal Spirit offered Himself without spot to God, cleanse your conscience from dead works to serve the living God? And for this reason He is the Mediator of the new covenant, by means of death, for the redemption of the transgressions under the first covenant, that those who are called may receive the promise of the eternal inheritance."

Hebrews 10:10–12 "By that will we have been sanctified through the offering of the body of Jesus Christ once for all. And every priest stands ministering daily and offering repeatedly the same sacrifices, which can never take away sins. But this Man, after He had offered one sacrifice for sins forever, sat down at the right hand of God..."

Hebrews 10:18–22 "Now where there is remission of these, there is no longer an offering for sin. Therefore, brethren, having boldness to enter the Holiest by the blood of Jesus, by a new and living way which He consecrated for us, through the veil, that is, His flesh, and having a High Priest over the house of God, let us draw near with a true heart in full assurance of faith, having our hearts sprinkled from the evil conscience and our bodies washed with pure water."

1 PETER

1 Peter 2:24 "...[W]ho Himself bore our sins in His own body on the tree, that we, having died to sins, might live for righteousness—by whose stripes you were healed."

1 Peter 3:18a "For Christ also suffered once for sins, the just for the unjust, that He might bring us to God..."

1 JOHN

1 John 4:10 "In this is love, not that we loved God, but that He loved us and sent His Son to be the propitiation for our sins."

1 John 4:15 "Whoever confesses that Jesus is the Son of God, God abides in him, and he in God."

1 John 5:1 "Whoever believes that Jesus is the Christ is born of God, and everyone who loves Him who begot also loves him who is begotten of Him."

REVELATION

Revelation 1:5b–6 "...To Him who loved us and washed us from our sins in His own blood and has made us kings and priests to His God and Father, to Him be glory and dominion forever and ever. Amen."

Revelation 5:6 "And I looked, and behold, in the midst of the throne and of the four living creatures, and in the midst of the elders, stood a Lamb as though it had been slain..."

Revelation 5:9b "...For You were slain, and have redeemed us to God by Your blood Out of every tribe and tongue and people and nation..."

Revelation 7:9–10 "After these things I looked, and behold, a great multitude which no one could number, of all nations, tribes, peoples, and tongues, standing before the throne and before the Lamb, clothed with white robes, with palm branches in their hands, and crying out with a loud voice, saying, 'Salvation belongs to our God who sits on the throne, and to the Lamb!'"

Revelation 12:10–11 "Then I heard a loud voice saying in heaven, 'Now salvation, and strength, and the kingdom of our God, and the power of His

Christ have come, for the accuser of our brethren, who accused them before our God day and night, has been cast down. And they overcame him by the blood of the Lamb and by the word of their testimony…"

The passages in Appendix C were taken from the NKJV.

CLOSING NOTE

If you have found this book helpful, please consider reviewing it. This will greatly help this book to reach new readers.

Thank you.